Legal Issues for Managers

Essential Skills for Avoiding Your Day in Court

Mike Deblieux

American Media Publishing

4900 University Avenue
West Des Moines, IA 50266-6769
800-262-2557

Legal Issues for Managers
Essential Skills for Avoiding Your Day in Court

Mike Deblieux

Credits:

American Media Publishing:	Arthur Bauer
	Todd McDonald
Project Manager:	Karen Massetti Miller
Designer:	Gayle O'Brien

Published by American Media Inc., 4900 University Avenue, West Des Moines, IA 50266-6769.
First Edition

Library of Congress Catalog Card Number 95-080142
Deblieux, Mike
Legal Issues for Managers: Essential Skills for Avoiding Your Day in Court

Printed in the United States of America
ISBN 1-884926-49-5

The AMI How-To Series

To obtain information about these and other AMI How-To Series books, please call: American Media Publishing at **800-262-2557.**

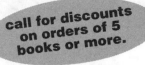

call for discounts on orders of 5 books or more.

TITLE	PRICE	QUANTITY	TOTAL
Assertiveness Skills Nelda Shelton and Sharon Burton	$12.95/ea.		
The Art of Giving and Receiving Feedback Shirley Poertner and Karen Massetti Miller	$12.95/ea.		
Attitude: The Choice Is Yours Michele Matt Yanna	$12.95/ea.		
Customer Service Excellence Debra J. MacNeill	$12.95/ea.		
Documenting Discipline Mike Deblieux	$12.95/ea.		
Effective Delegation Skills Bruce B. Tepper	$12.95/ea.		
Effective Teamwork Michael D. Maginn	$12.95/ea.		
High Impact Presentations Robert W. Pike, CSP	$12.95/ea.		
The Human Touch Performance Appraisal Charles M. Cadwell	$12.95/ea.		
I Have to Fire Someone! Richard S. Deems, Ph.D.	$12.95/ea.		
Interviewing: More Than A Gut Feeling Richard S. Deems, Ph.D.	$12.95/ea.		
Investing Time For Maximum Return Melody Mackenzie and Alec Mackenzie	$12.95/ea.		
Keep Them Calling! **Superior Service on the Telephone** Sherry L. Barrett	$12.95/ea.		
Leading Teams: The Skills For Success Sam R. Lloyd	$12.95/ea.		
Listen Up: Hear What's Really Being Said Jim Dugger	$12.95/ea.		
Job Strategies for New Employees Robert Lucas	$12.95/ea.		
Making Change Work For You! Richard S. Deems, Ph.D.F	$12.95/ea.		
Making Meetings Work Karen Anderson	$12.95/ea.		
Managing Conflict at Work Jim Murphy	$12.95/ea.		
Managing Stress Kristine C. Brewer	$12.95/ea.		
Negotiate With Confidence Ed Brodow	$12.95/ea.		
The New Supervisor: Skills for Success Bruce B. Tepper	$12.95/ea.		
Positive Mental Attitude in the Workplace Marian Thomas	$12.95/ea.		
Self-Esteem: The Power to Be Your Best Marc Towers	$12.95/ea.		
Sold on Selling: Skills and Techniques Doug Malouf	$12.95/ea.		
Ten Tools for Quality Richard Chang, Ph.D.	$12.95/ea.		
Training That Works! Charles M. Cadwell	$12.95/ea.		
Why Didn't I Think of That? Lee Towe	$12.95/ea.		
Writing for Business Results Patricia E. Seraydarian	$12.95/ea.		
Legal Issues for Managers Mike Deblieux	$12.95/ea.		
Shipping and handling will be added to your order.	**TOTAL**		

BEST SELLER (Documenting Discipline)

BEST SELLER (The Human Touch Performance Appraisal)

BEST SELLER (Interviewing: More Than A Gut Feeling)

NEW (Keep Them Calling!)

NEW (Why Didn't I Think of That?)

NEW (Legal Issues for Managers)

Four Easy Ways To Order

- **CALL:** 800-262-2557

- **FAX:** 515-224-0256

- **MAIL:** American Media Incorporated
  4900 University Avenue
  West Des Moines, Iowa
  50266-6769

- **E-MAIL:** AMI@ammedia.com

Name _____

Title _____

Organization _____

Address _____

City _____

State/Zip _____

Daytime Phone (_____) _____

FAX _____

Method of Payment

☐ I've enclosed check # _____
  payable to American Media Inc.

☐ Credit Card — Charge my order,
  plus shipping and handling to my credit card.

☐ Mastercard ☐ VISA ☐ American Express

[MasterCard] [VISA] [AMERICAN EXPRESS]

Exp. Date | MO. | YR. |

CARD NO.

☐☐☐☐ - ☐☐☐☐ - ☐☐☐☐ - ☐☐☐☐

Signature _____

This page is reproducible
for easy reference and faxing.

Introduction

Employment practices in the United States are governed by a wide variety of federal, state, and local laws. As a supervisor, you must understand these laws so that you can make objective, consistent, and legal decisions. You do not have to be an expert on every aspect of every employment law, but you do have to know enough to recognize when you need to seek help from a human resources professional or legal counsel.

Some supervisors make light of their responsibility to comply with the law. Others use excuses to justify, in their own minds, how the law does not apply to them. In the end, they pay a heavy price in low employee morale or in hours of depositions, hearings, and other legal proceedings.

As a consultant, I have traveled across the United States for much of the last ten years helping managers, supervisors, and human resources advisors to understand their responsibility to manage effectively within the context of legal requirements. This book is based on the experience of interacting with thousands of workshop participants who want to understand, apply, and comply with the law. *Legal Issues for Managers: Essential Skills for Avoiding Your Day in Court* will show you how employment law affects your ability to be an effective supervisor. It is written from a human resources perspective and will help you discuss personnel issues with other supervisors, managers, and human resources professionals.

Legal Issues for Managers will not help you make specific personnel decisions. Each personnel decision involves a wide variety of variables—your manager, your human resources advisors, and your legal counsel can help you consider the legal requirements that apply to specific situations. Consider this book a starting point to help you begin to understand a complex array of concepts.

Mike Deblieux

What You Will Gain from Reading This Book

As a manager or supervisor, you must be knowledgeable in a variety of areas. You must know a great deal about your own area of expertise and have an understanding of customer service, budgets, and safety. You must also know how to manage people effectively.

Managing people effectively includes understanding how a wide variety of laws affect you, your company, and the employees who work for you. You cannot make decisions based only on your personal opinions and feelings. Your decisions must be objective and fair, and they must be based upon what is right for you, your company, and the employees. Your decisions must also minimize legal exposure and liability for you and your company. This book has been written to help you learn how to make such decisions.

After reading this book and completing the exercises it contains, you should be able to:

- Recognize when you are making a decision that is affected by a major federal employment law.
- Recognize when you need to seek the advice of a human resources professional or a legal advisor.
- Help other employees and supervisors understand their roles in ensuring that your organization complies with various employment laws.

You may have some additional goals of your own. Take a minute to list them here:

_____

_____

_____

About the Author

Mike Deblieux is a nationally recognized human resources management trainer and consultant. He is president of Mike Deblieux Human Resources in Tustin, California. He designs and presents training programs on human resources-related issues such as Documenting Discipline, Writing Performance Reviews, Interviewing, Preventing Sexual Harassment, Equal Employment Opportunity, Affirmative Action, and Workplace Violence. He writes and updates employee handbooks and personnel policy manuals and also provides a full range of HR consulting services to organizations of all sizes.

Mike is an Instructor for the University of California, Irvine, Extension Human Resources Management Certificate Program and was recently presented the Extension's Distinguished Instructor Award. He is also a Course Leader and Blue Ribbon Speaker for the American Management Association (AMA). He is also a course leader for The Employers Group and the Professionals in Human Resources Association (PIHRA).

Mike has recently written *Documenting Discipline* for American Media Publishing. American Media Incorporated has produced a training video, *Documenting Discipline,* based on his book. The book and the video may be ordered by calling 800-262-2557. Mike can be reached at 714-669-0309 or by E-mail at MDHR@aol.com

Acknowledgments

The author wishes to thank Art Bauer and Todd McDonald at American Media for their help, support, and assistance on this book. Thanks and appreciation are extended to Lee Paterson, Attorney at Law, and Teresa Tracy, Attorney at Law, for their roles as mentors and friends. Special thanks also go to Joan, Danielle, Nicole, Molly, and Sarah for their patience and support during the time it took to work on this and other projects. And thank you to Karen Nichols for learning the word processor, HR, and my many quirks to bring this project to completion.

Book Objectives

Reading a book is an investment of your time. You should be sure that you receive a good return on your investment. This book is organized to help you maximize your investment. **Chapter Objectives** tell you what you will learn in each chapter. **Self-Check** sections are included throughout the book to help you implement the information you learn. **For Your Information** sections appear in several places to provide additional ideas to help you understand the topics discussed in this book. Key words are highlighted in *italics*. Their definitions are listed in the **Glossary** in the back of the book. A **Chapter Review** section is included at the end of each chapter to help you reinforce what you learn. We hope these additional tools help you to make the best possible investment of your time.

Gender/Ethnic References

This is a book about equal opportunity and fairness in the workplace. Men and women work side by side in the workplace, as do people representing many different cultures, races, colors, and religions.

The author has worked to reflect this diversity in two ways. From a gender perspective, the text alternates between using "he" and "she" in examples. In some situations, the phrase "he or she" or "she or he" is used. From an ethnic perspective, a variety of culturally diverse names have been used in the text. We hope this approach helps enrich your appreciation of the diversity of the American workplace.

Why Learn About Employment Law?

Chapter Objectives

After reading this chapter and completing the exercises, you should be able to:

 Explain why your job as a supervisor depends on your studying and learning more about employment law.

 Explain why personnel decisions must take into consideration potential legal consequences.

 List three basic steps you can take to minimize liability for your organization.

For Your Information

As you read through this book, you will see individual words or phrases in *italics*. These are key words that you should add to your vocabulary. They are listed in the Glossary at the back of the book.

Jessica couldn't believe it. An employee she'd fired six months ago was suing the company—and her! For the past two weeks, it seemed that all she'd done was talk to attorneys, and they were asking for all sorts of documentation that she just didn't have. "What about the new product?" she asked her manager. "It's been my project from Day 1. We'll be ready to introduce it in a few weeks."

"Someone else will have to take over for you," her manager said, shaking his head. "You'll be spending the next few months in court."

These days, nearly every newspaper or news broadcast has a story about an employee lawsuit. Today's employees understand that they have rights at work, and they are not afraid to exercise those rights, often with the help of an attorney.

The Cost of a Lawsuit

Newspaper and television reports measure the cost of a lawsuit in terms of the final judgment. (In 1994, for example, the average California jury verdict in employment cases was $1,924,007.) Unfortunately, the final judgment seldom tells the "real" cost of a lawsuit. The real cost includes time, lost productivity, attorneys' fees, and court costs. There are also personal, emotional, and physical health costs that can rarely be measured in terms of dollars and cents.

Once a lawsuit has been filed, you have little control over the cost. But you can control legal expenses by managing people in a manner that prevents lawsuits. This includes using job-related criteria to hire, promote, evaluate, and discipline employees and being fair and consistent in each of your personnel decisions.

The Supervisor Is the Company

As a supervisor, you represent your company to each employee on your team. You explain company policies and procedures and make decisions about work assignments, hours, and pay. When you communicate clearly, the company communicates clearly, but when your message is unclear or when you are seen as unfair or inconsistent, employees see the company that way too.

Employees use a simple phrase to describe what they want from supervisors and managers: *"Walk the talk."* This means, *"Do what you said you were going to do."* The company says what it is going to do in a number of ways. Employee handbooks, policy manuals, annual reports, and speeches by the CEO frequently boast that employees are a company's most important asset. These and other pieces of communication often promise employees fair treatment and a great work environment. When a supervisor does not come through on these promises, employees become disillusioned, and that disillusionment plants the seeds for lawsuits.

In your role as supervisor, you must *walk the talk*. You must go out of your way to set an example of fairness and send employees a message that the company cares about them. When employees believe that they work for a company that has their best interests at heart, they do not seek outside counsel, and they do not sue.

1

Once a lawsuit has been filed, you have little control over the cost. But you can control legal expenses by managing people in a manner that prevents lawsuits.

Addressing Employee Problems and Concerns

"I don't know how I'm going to do it," Carmen thought as she read the memo on her new job assignment. She was being transferred from the branch where she currently worked to the one across town. The extra commute time would make it impossible for her to pick up her children before their day care closed. "I wish there were some way I could complain," she said to herself, "but I don't think my supervisor would even listen to me. I wonder if there's some sort of legal action I can take?"

How can Carmen's employers address her concerns?

Every organization should provide the means for employees to bring their problems and concerns to the attention of management before an employee feels the need to seek outside counsel. This can be done by establishing formal grievance and complaint procedures.

A *grievance procedure* provides a way for employees to ask for and receive a timely review of a management decision or action. (Two examples of potential grievances are a transfer to another work location that is undesirable to the employee or the amount of a merit increase.) A grievance procedure usually has at least three steps, including:

> **Step 1:** Supervisor reviews the employee's grievance.
>
> **Step 2:** If the employee is not satisfied with the supervisor's answer, she may appeal to a manager.
>
> **Step 3:** If the employee is not satisfied with the manager's answer, she may appeal to a higher-level manager, such as the CEO or Director of Human Resources. The decision of the person at this level is final.

The managers involved in processing a grievance must carefully consider what the employee has to say. They must present the management side of the story in a careful, factual manner. The person who makes a final decision about a grievance must review all the information that is presented, and she must make a fair and objective decision.

A *grievance procedure* provides a way for employees to ask for and receive a timely review of a management decision or action.

✔ Self-Check

Does your organization have a grievance procedure? If it does, what steps does it include? If it does not, can you determine the reason why it doesn't?

_____

_____

_____

_____

Another way to ensure that employees take their problems and concerns to management is to have a well-publicized *complaint procedure*. A complaint procedure is similar to a grievance procedure, but it does not have steps. The employee uses the complaint procedure to bring a problem to management's attention, and it is management's responsibility to investigate the matter, determine if a problem exists, and resolve it. Sexual harassment is an example of a problem an employee would submit to a complaint procedure.

Human Resources

Your Human Resources Department (in some companies, it's called Personnel) is a valuable resource. Human resources (HR) professionals are trained to advise you on how to handle employee problems. Allowing HR professionals to be an integral part of your team can help you minimize legal exposure.

Your HR advisor helps other managers with their problems and knows how the company has handled employee issues similar to yours. Her advice can help you be consistent in the way you interpret and apply policies, procedures, discipline, and other management tools.

💡 For Your Information

A complaint procedure must give an employee an alternative of whom to go to for help. For example, an employee would usually take a workplace problem to her supervisor. However, if the problem is sexual harassment, and the supervisor is doing the harassing, the supervisor would be the wrong person to receive the complaint. Your procedure must allow the employee to go to a manager or to human resources to submit a complaint. It should also allow the employee to choose between a man and a woman to receive the complaint.

HR can also serve as an independent, objective third party to help you resolve problems. HR representatives can facilitate a discussion between you and an employee. They can witness disciplinary action meetings and can also conduct independent investigations into employee performance problems.

In most companies, HR is your link to legal counsel. Because legal advice is expensive, you cannot call an attorney for every problem. When you do call an attorney, you should be ready with enough information to allow the attorney to give you competent advice. Your HR representative can help you organize your information and thoughts before you meet with the attorney.

Legal Advisors

In addition to human resources advisors, you should have access to the advice and services of a qualified labor attorney. Though you generally will not have day-to-day contact with your company's labor attorney, it is important for you to get to know her. If you ever do need to work with her, a thorough, candid discussion of the issues will be crucial to resolving the problem at its earliest stage. If you are uncomfortable or intimidated, you will have difficulty being a full partner in the discussion.

The role of your labor attorney is to help you apply the law to a specific situation. The attorney must help you to understand what you can and cannot say and do within that situation. She must also decide what, if any, court papers need to be filed. Ultimately, the attorney will represent the company, and possibly you, in court.

Attorneys operate on the basis of a concept called *attorney-client privilege*. This means that you can talk with your attorney confidentially. There can be exceptions to this rule; your attorney will explain them to you when they apply. For our purposes, it is important for you to understand that the attorney-client privilege is designed to give you every opportunity to share information, positive or negative, with your labor attorney so that she may fully represent the company and you.

Attorneys operate on the basis of a concept called *attorney-client privilege*. This means that you can talk with your attorney confidentially.

14

It's Your Decision

Despite all the advice available to you, you are ultimately responsible for supervising the employees in your work unit. Human Resources, the company attorney, or even this book cannot make your decisions for you.

Whether or not you make the right decision may not be apparent for weeks, months, or even years. Ultimately, however, your chances of making the right decision improve when you carefully weigh the circumstances of a specific situation against your legal obligations and the advice of various experts, with a goal of being fair and equitable to both the company and the employee.

Despite all the advice available to you, you are ultimately responsible for supervising the employees in your work unit.

1

Steps for the Effective Supervisor

Here are some suggestions to help you implement the information in this chapter. If you use them, they will help you avoid legal problems. They will also help you manage people in a way that shows you respect them and appreciate their efforts and contributions.

Step 1— Read one chapter of a book each day. This book has eight chapters. If you read one chapter of a book like this each day, you will read 45.6 books in a year. (OK, so you take a day off every once in a while. You're still going to read a lot more than anyone else.) Pick different topics—read about performance reviews, customer service, finance, psychology, and other business issues. As your knowledge grows, your skill as a supervisor will grow.

Step 2— Learn to communicate effectively. Speak clearly and at a level the other person will understand. Write in the same way you talk—use short, direct sentences. Most important, listen to what other people say to you. Ask them questions to be sure you understand what they are saying.

Step 3—Find out if your organization has a grievance or complaint procedure. Read it. Ask questions about it. Explain the procedure to employees. Encourage them to come to you with their problems, but also make sure they understand that the grievance procedure is available for them to use.

Step 4—Get to know your human resources representative. Go visit her or invite her to visit your department. The more you know about each other, the easier it will be for you to work together on tough employee relations issues.

Step 5—Keep accurate records about work and employment issues in your department. They will help you be a better supervisor. They will also help you explain what actually happened in the event of a lawsuit or other legal claim.

Chapter One Review

Now that you have read Chapter One, use this space to review what you have learned so far. If you are not sure of an answer, just refer to the text. **Answers appear on page 112.**

1. A supervisor must be fair and consistent because:
   a. Fair and consistent supervisors are less likely to be sued.
   b. The law requires it.
   c. It makes employees happy.

2. To an employee, a supervisor is the company because:

   _____

   _____

   _____

3. Two effective ways to prevent lawsuits include:

   a. _____

   b. _____

4. As a supervisor, you should include Human Resources on your team because:
   a. HR is a necessary evil.
   b. HR can advise you on how to handle a variety of situations.
   c. The company president thinks it's a good idea.

5. Attorney-client privilege gives you the right to:

   _____

   _____

   _____

CHAPTER TWO

Equal Employment

Chapter Objectives

After reading this chapter and completing the exercises, you should be able to:

 List the groups protected from discrimination by the Civil Rights Act of 1964 and its amendments.

 Explain three types of discrimination: disparate treatment, disparate impact, and retaliation.

 Define the term job-related.

Ed slammed the newspaper down in disgust. "I'm sick of all these people demanding special privileges," he groaned. "Pretty soon, the rest of us won't have any rights left at all!"

Equal employment is one of our most important legal concepts. Federal, state, and local laws prohibit *discrimination* in employment practices. They require supervisors and managers to make employment decisions without regard to an individual's membership in a wide variety of *protected groups,* such as age, race, religion, or sex. Contrary to popular belief, equal employment is not limited to a few people. Virtually every applicant, employee, and former employee is protected from discrimination based on one or more protected groups.

> **Virtually every applicant, employee, and former employee is protected from *discrimination* based on one or more protected groups.**

The Civil Rights Act of 1964 and Its Amendments
Establishing Equal Employment

The Civil Rights Act of 1964 is the most widely known equal employment law. The employment section of the Civil Rights Act of 1964 is called **Title VII.** It prohibits discrimination based on race, color, religion, sex, and national origin. The law applies to all private sector employers with 15 or more employees. It also applies to labor unions.

The Civil Rights Act of 1964 created the **Equal Employment Opportunity Commission (EEOC).** The EEOC is responsible for enforcing Title VII. The EEOC can receive and investigate complaints. Claims must be filed with the EEOC within 180 days of an incident.

✔ Self-Check

The Civil Rights Act is a federal law. Your state may also have laws that prevent discrimination. Take a moment to find a state discrimination poster in your employee break room and see if it lists groups that are protected from discrimination that are not covered by the Civil Rights Act. Keep in mind that occasionally, a state law may require you to do more than a federal law. List the groups protected by state laws in your state below:

_____

_____

_____

_____

Expanding Coverage

The Civil Rights Act of 1964 was amended in 1972 by the **Equal Employment Opportunity Act.** This law extended the coverage of Title VII beyond private sector employers and labor unions to include state and local government agencies as well as public and private educational institutions. The 1972 amendments also expanded the authority of the EEOC by allowing it to file suit in the federal courts against employers.

Protecting Pregnancy

In 1978, the Civil Rights Act was amended by the **Pregnancy Discrimination Act.** This law prohibits discrimination based on pregnancy, childbirth, or related medical conditions. It requires employers to offer leaves of absence, insurance, and on-the-job accommodations for pregnancy in the same way they accommodate other medical conditions.

Jury Trials and Damages

The Civil Rights Act of 1991 added some important provisions to the process of prohibiting discrimination in the workplace. Besides enforcement by the EEOC, the law allows jury trials and punitive and compensatory damages that were not previously available. In cases of intentional discrimination, the amount of damages can be as much as $300,000 depending on the size of the employer.

Civil Rights Act of 1964 and Its Amendments

Civil Rights Act of 1964 .... Title VII prohibits discrimination based on race, color, religion, sex, and national origin. Applies to private sector employers with 15 or more employees, and labor unions.

Equal Employment Opportunity Act (1972).............. Extends Title VII coverage to include state and local government agencies, and public and private educational institutions.

Pregnancy Discrimination Act (1978) .... Prohibits discrimination based on pregnancy, childbirth, and related medical conditions.

Civil Rights Act of 1991 .... Allows for jury trials and punitive and compensatory damages.

Employees	Damages Limitations
1–14	No damages. Damages may be available under state law.
15–100	up to $50,000
101–200	up to $100,000
201–500	up to $200,000
500+	up to $300,000

What Is Employment Discrimination?

Employment discrimination often occurs when subjective decisions are made about people in the workplace. Managers typically make a variety of *employment decisions,* including:

- Hiring and promotion
- Discipline and termination
- Assigning work and responsibilities
- Training, coaching, and counseling
- Establishing terms (length) of employment
- Establishing conditions of employment
- Establishing privileges (benefits) of employment

These and other employment decisions must be based on *job-related* information. A job-related decision is based on objective criteria that are directly linked to doing the work that needs to be done. Consider the following example:

You need to leave someone in charge while you are on vacation. You have a choice between Danielle and Maria.

Danielle has been taking leadership classes. She makes good business decisions. She volunteered to be a team leader to help implement the new computer system. Other team members reported that they liked working under her leadership.

Employment discrimination often occurs when subjective decisions are made about people in the workplace.

21

Maria is your best friend. You want to see her get ahead in her career. Despite your encouragement, Maria has not taken classes. Her attendance record is below average, and she is late on a report that should have been turned in last week.

Whom should you leave in charge?

If you pick Danielle, you are using business reasons for your decision; therefore, your decision is objective. If you pick Maria, you are using emotion and friendship; therefore, your decision is subjective. Your employment decisions must be objective decisions.

✔ Self-Check

Many of today's workers (maybe you are one of them) were born after the Civil Rights Act of 1964 was passed. It is interesting and educational to talk with the people who were in the workforce before the Civil Rights Act. As you read this chapter, take some time to talk with someone who was working before 1964. Your parents or grandparents might be good resources. Here are some possible questions for you to ask:

✔ Prior to 1978, what rights did a working woman have on the job when she became pregnant?

✔ Prior to 1964, what percentage of your workforce was Black? Hispanic? Asian? Native American?

✔ What impact did the Civil Rights Act have on your career? Your organization?

Three Types of Employment Discrimination

The Equal Employment Opportunity Commission and the courts have defined three types of employment discrimination:

- **Disparate treatment**
- **Disparate impact**
- **Retaliation**

Disparate Treatment

Disparate treatment discrimination is intentional. It occurs when:

- A person is treated differently from others.

- The different treatment is based on that person's race, color, sex, religion, national origin, or another protected category.

- The different treatment is on purpose.

You are interviewing Rahsaan and Alanna for an open position. Your first interview is with Rahsaan. You ask him ten job-related questions. Rahsaan provides good answers and you consider him a strong candidate. When Rahsaan leaves, Alanna comes in for her interview. You ask Alanna the same ten questions you asked Rahsaan, but you also ask Alanna an eleventh question, "Do you have children?"

Could your question to Alanna be considered disparate treatment?

Clearly, you treated Alanna differently than you treated Rahsaan. You asked her the question to get an answer. The implication is that you wanted the answer to help you decide which candidate to hire. A reasonable conclusion is that you treated Alanna differently because she is a woman. Your treatment was intentional. Alanna is a victim of disparate treatment discrimination.

For Your Information

Title VII of the Civil Rights Act defines an employer as any employer with more than 15 employees, and any agent of such an employer. Some courts have held that a supervisor is an agent of the employer. As an agent of the employer, a supervisor can be sued and held personally liable for discrimination.

Disparate impact **discrimination occurs when a decision, practice, or policy has a disproportionately negative effect on a protected group.**

Disparate Impact

Disparate impact discrimination may be unintentional. It occurs when a decision, practice, or policy has a disproportionately negative effect on a protected group.

Before the Civil Rights Act of 1964, many fire departments required firefighter applicants to be at least 5-feet-10-inches tall and to weigh at least 165 pounds. The reason for this requirement was to ensure that strong, physically fit people were hired as firefighters. However, height and weight do not always show that a person is strong. Because of these requirements, women, Hispanics, Filipinos, Asians, and others who were strong and physically fit were not considered for the job of firefighter.

Were fire departments intentionally discriminating against these groups?

Whether fire departments meant to discriminate or not, there was a disproportionately negative impact on employment opportunities for women and certain minorities in fire departments. As a result, a number of protected groups were victims of disparate impact discrimination.

Retaliation

Retaliation discrimination occurs when one person takes action against another person who has exercised his or her right to complain about discrimination. Retaliation is frequently intentional and vindictive.

Letticia files a discrimination claim with Human Resources based on her gender and national origin. Her complaint is about a promotion she did not receive. It is based on a decision her supervisor, Manfred, made to promote John. When Manfred learns that Letticia has filed the complaint, he stops talking to her. He also begins giving her lower-level, repetitive work assignments. When he learns that Maria has offered to support Letticia by serving as a witness in the investigation, he begins to give Maria lower-level work assignments also.

Retaliation **discrimination occurs when one person takes action against another person who has exercised his or her right to complain about discrimination.**

Has Manfred discriminated against Letticia and Maria?

Letticia and Maria are both involved in exercising Letticia's right to ask for a review, based on antidiscrimination laws, of Manfred's decision to promote John. Manfred is holding that right against both of them; therefore, Manfred is retaliating.

A Management Perspective

The law clearly prohibits discrimination. But there are other reasons to avoid such practices as well. Our society is becoming increasingly diverse. This diversity is reflected in your employees, your customers, and the community in which you do business. Despite your personal feelings about diversity, it is here to stay. Your organization's success depends on productive employees, satisfied clients, and a good relationship with the diverse community in which you do business.

An employee who feels he is being treated differently (because of race, color, gender, religion, or some other factor) is not a productive employee. A customer who feels slighted or mistreated because of his ethnicity is not likely to return. A community group that senses your organization is not open to minorities and women is unlikely to refer its members to you or to ask you to participate in its activities. In short, it is in your best interest as a member of the business community to ensure that your organization is open to people of all backgrounds, cultures, and interests.

Your organization's success depends on productive employees, satisfied clients, and a good relationship with the diverse community in which you do business.

✔ Self-Check

How diverse is your workplace? Here is a partial list of factors that make the American workplace diverse. Check those that apply to your workplace and add others that you can think of.

- ❏ Race
- ❏ National Origin
- ❏ Gender
- ❏ Education
- ❏ Pregnancy
- ❏ Sexual Orientation
- ❏ Language
- ❏ Religion
- ❏ Color
- ❏ Age
- ❏ Disability
- ❏ Single Parent
- ❏ Military Service

Steps for the Effective Supervisor

Here are some suggestions to help you implement the information in this chapter. If you use them, they will help you avoid legal problems. They will also help you manage people in a way that shows you respect them and appreciate their efforts and contributions.

Step 1—Ask your corporate labor attorney to give you an actual discrimination court case summary to read. Reading a case from an appellate court or the Supreme Court can help you understand how the law is interpreted and applied.

Step 2—Call your local office of the Equal Employment Opportunity Commission or your state employment commission. Ask them to send you a copy of their brochures on discrimination in the workplace.

Step 3—Make sure that you have a specific, job-related reason for each employment decision you make.

Step 4—Take a course to learn more about cultural diversity. Learn more about the values, customs, and practices of the people you work with every day.

Chapter Two Review

Now that you have read Chapter Two, use this space to review what you have learned so far. If you are not sure of an answer, just refer to the text. **Answers appear on page 112.**

1. The Civil Rights Act of 1964 prohibits discrimination on the basis of:

   _____

   _____

   _____

2. The term *protected group* means:

   _____

   _____

3. The Civil Rights Act of 1964 was amended in 1972, 1978, and 1991. What was the key provision of each amendment?

   1972 _____

   1978 _____

   1991 _____

4. *Disparate treatment discrimination* is:

   _____

5. *Disparate impact discrimination* is:

   _____

6. *Retaliation* is:

   _____

7. A *job-related decision* is:

   _____

CHAPTER THREE

Harassment and Sexual Harassment

Chapter Objectives

After reading this chapter and completing the exercises, you should be able to:

 Explain the concepts of verbal, physical, and visual harassment.

 Explain the concepts of quid pro quo and environmental sexual harassment.

 List several steps to prevent harassment and sexual harassment.

"How do you like your new job in the parts department?" Ingrid asked Rita.

"I like the work, but I don't really feel comfortable there," Rita answered sadly. "I'm the only woman in the department, and the men who work there like to hang up a lot of swimsuit pictures. Maybe I should transfer back to word processing."

Harassment and sexual harassment are two of the most discussed topics in human resources. They are forms of discrimination. Harassment can be directed against any *protected group*. Sexual harassment is a form of sex discrimination. Harassment and sexual harassment can be intentional or unintentional.

What Is Harassment?

Harassment means to disturb, torment, or pester on a persistent basis.

Harassment means to disturb, torment, or pester on a persistent basis. Harassment can occur in many different forms. Some harassment can be legitimate or lawful. An employee may believe that a supervisor who frequently asks about the status of an important report is "harassing" him. But since the supervisor has a legitimate business reason for the question, it would not be considered unlawful harassment.

When we talk about unlawful harassment in the workplace, we are talking about people being treated inappropriately because of their membership in one or more protected groups. Usually, our membership in a protected group is not optional. A 45-year-old African-American female is a natural member of three protected groups: age, race, and gender. Sometimes, though, membership in a protected group is voluntary. Religion is an example of this type of protected group.

Whether your membership in a protected group is natural or voluntary, you most likely take your membership in the group seriously. If someone uses your membership against you or makes fun of it, you will be hurt or offended. You will likely say that you have been harassed.

The three most frequently discussed types of illegal harassment are:

- ■ **Verbal**

- ■ **Physical**

- ■ **Visual**

You must be aware of the many different forms these types of harassment can take and be prepared to address them in whatever form they occur.

Verbal Harassment

Verbal harassment includes spoken words, written words, and sounds that people make. When these words and sounds are directed toward other people in a way that disturbs, torments, or pesters them based on their membership in a protected group, they are very likely a victim of verbal harassment. Verbal harassment becomes illegal harassment when it is unwelcome and unreasonable.

For Your Information

Some people think that the issues of harassment and sexual harassment have been blown out of proportion. In reality, it is astonishing how many people have a personal experience with harassment and sexual harassment. Ask someone you know well (maybe a family member or close friend) if she or he has been a victim of harassment or sexual harassment. (Be sensitive to the other person's feelings. If she or he does not want to discuss the experience, express your respect for his or her feelings and move the conversation to another subject.) Ask this person if she or he filed a complaint. Ask if he or she would do anything different today.

Verbal harassment can take the form of an *epithet*. An epithet is a word that labels or stereotypes a person or group based on membership in one or more protected categories. Epithets are often used in anger or frustration. They are sometimes used to put people down or make them look bad to others. Sometimes epithets are used as a term of endearment or to be cute or funny. Sometimes they are used out of ignorance. Whatever their purpose, epithets label or stereotype the person or group toward which they are directed.

✔ Self-Check

One of the more difficult challenges of harassment and sexual harassment is for people to unlearn old habits. Many people do and say things because they have always done them. As the workforce changes, those old habits become less and less acceptable. Think about some of your old habits and ask yourself if any of them could be offensive to other people. Watch your friends at work this week. Can you help one of them avoid a problem by pointing out an old habit that others might misinterpret?

Most epithets are easy to recognize and are known to be inappropriate in the workplace. However, different people view words in different ways. What is an epithet to one person might be just a descriptive word to another.

Would you consider this statement to include an epithet?

Mario speaking to Zhang: "Get one of the girls to take care of it."

Many people would consider the use of the word "girls" to imply a subservient or second-class role for women in the workplace. When used in this context, they would consider the word "girls" to be an epithet.

By contrast, would you consider this statement to contain an epithet?

Nicole speaking to Alison: "Let's get the girls together and go to lunch."

When women use the term "girls" to refer to other women, it is often considered a term of friendship, not an epithet. In the workplace, this creates a particularly difficult dilemma. If men are told that the word is inappropriate, but then hear women using it to describe themselves, they can become confused. To avoid the problem, all employees should be encouraged to refer to other people by their names, job titles, or departments. For example, Mario could say to Zhang:

"Ask Maria to take care of it for us."

Nicole could say to Alison:

"Let's see if Claire, Espe, and Chidzigyak want to go to lunch."

Another form of verbal harassment is a derogatory comment. A derogatory comment puts down a person or group or belittles them. For example, "You stupid [racial group]s are all the same." Clearly, such a statement is inappropriate.

Yet another form of verbal harassment is a slur. A slur is a change in a person's normal speech pattern to imply something about another person or group based on membership in a protected category. Mimicking an accent or speech impediment might be a slur based on national origin or a disability. Lisping words to imply something about another person's sexual orientation could be a slur based on gender. Whistling, grunting, groaning, or any number of other noises directed toward another person could be considered a slur based on a several protected categories.

Physical Harassment

Physical harassment includes, but is not limited to, assault, impeding or blocking movement, or any physical interference with normal work or movement directed at an individual. For example, hitting, pushing, or knocking someone down would be considered physical harassment. Blocking the way of someone in a corridor to force that person to go to the other side of the corridor or turn around would be physical harassment. Actions that were once considered horseplay may now be considered harassment. For example, putting petroleum jelly on a steering wheel would be physical harassment if it is directed at the person because she or he is a member of a protected group. Another form of physical harassment is inappropriate touching. Placing a hand on another person's buttocks, breasts, or crotch would clearly be a form of physical harassment. A more subtle, but equally inappropriate, form of physical harassment would be frequently touching another person on the shoulder (or any other place) against that person's wishes, purposely brushing up against another person while walking or passing by, or moving a leg toward the leg of another person under a table to make contact.

✔ Self-Check

What would you do if you saw someone touch an employee in an inappropriate or offensive manner? Since it is your responsibility as a supervisor to create a positive, harassment-free environment, you should confront the person and, if necessary, take disciplinary action.

What would you do if someone told an offensive or vulgar joke at work? One thing you *should* do is avoid laughing or responding to the joke. You should also decide whether counseling or discipline is appropriate to clearly communicate that the company prohibits such behavior.

Visual Harassment

Visual harassment includes, but is not limited to, pictures, posters, calendars, cartoons, statements written on walls, and other objects that can be clearly seen. Pinups or calendars featuring scantily clad men or women fall into this category. Cartoons, posters, and other pictures that depict minorities or women in a demeaning or derogatory manner are considered visual harassment. Statements written on bathroom walls and company posters defaced in a racial, sexual, or other derogatory manner would also be considered visual harassment.

Recently, companies have begun to deal with new forms of visual harassment related to the computer. One example is "screen savers" depicting scantily clad or nude people. Another example is the exchange or delivery of racial, suggestive, lewd, or even pornographic E-mail messages or pictures.

Visual harassment includes, but is not limited to, pictures, posters, calendars, cartoons, statements written on walls, and other objects that can be clearly seen.

What Is Sexual Harassment?

Sexual harassment includes behavior such as unwelcome sexual advances, requests for sexual favors, and other verbal or physical conduct of a sexual nature, such as name-calling, suggestive comments, or lewd talk and jokes.

Sexual harassment often takes one of two forms:

- **Quid pro quo harassment**

- **Environmental harassment**

Quid Pro Quo

Quid pro quo means "something for something" or "this for that." In other words, "If you do something for me, I'll do something for you." Quid pro quo sexual harassment occurs when one person is asked, forced, pressured, or influenced to provide sexual favors or acts as a *term, condition, or privilege of employment.*

Quid pro quo sexual harassment is normally a result of a lead worker, team leader, supervisor, or manager using his or her power or authority in an inappropriate way to gain a sexual advantage over an employee. In fact, in one case, a court used the term "extortion" to describe quid pro quo sexual harassment.

Quid pro quo sexual harassment could be as blatant as a supervisor telling an employee that she or he must have sex with him or her to get a raise. It might be as subtle as a supervisor resting a hand on the shoulder of an employee in a suggestive manner at every opportunity. Regardless of the actual form it takes, quid pro quo sexual harassment places the employee in the position of having to choose between continuing to work under the existing conditions or filing a complaint. The courts hold companies and supervisors *strictly liable* for quid pro quo harassment. Strictly liable means that there is no excuse for the behavior. If quid pro quo harassment is found to exist, the company and the supervisor will pay a heavy price.

For Your Information

Employers must take sexual harassment claims seriously. They must conduct a prompt and thorough investigation of complaints and implement timely and effective corrective action to eliminate harassment. An effective investigation considers:

- **The Totality of the Circumstances**—the nature of the conduct, the context of the events, the severity and pervasiveness of the behavior, whether it was threatening or humiliating, whether it was unwelcome, and whether it unreasonably interfered with the individual's work performance.

- **Reasonableness**—whether a reasonable person in the same or similar circumstances would view the behavior as harassment.

- **Hostility**—whether the person filing the complaint considered the behavior to be hostile or abusive.

Quid pro quo sexual harassment **could be as blatant as a supervisor telling an employee that she or he must have sex with him or her to get a raise.**

Environmental Sexual Harassment

Environmental sexual harassment occurs when workplace conduct unreasonably interferes with an individual's work performance or creates an intimidating, hostile, or offensive work environment. Environmental sexual harassment can be intentional or unintentional. Companies are liable for environmental sexual harassment when they *knew or should have known* that it was taking place.

Environmental sexual harassment can and often does occur between coworkers. It can also involve supervisors and managers. Environmental sexual harassment can be verbal, physical, or visual. When it is present, the workplace environment is—at best—uncomfortable, and—at worst—intolerable.

Environmental sexual harassment occurs when:

■ A sexual joke is told in the workplace.

■ People use nicknames like "babe," "honey," "hunk," or "sweetheart."

■ Two coworkers who are dating outside the workplace bring their relationship into the workplace in a manner that makes it difficult for others to interact with one or both of them.

■ Suggestive pictures, posters, or calendars are displayed in the workplace. One person looks at another in a way that causes the second person to feel as though he or she has been "undressed" with the eyes of the first person. A customer makes suggestive, rude, or crude remarks to an employee.

■ The employees of an outside vendor use vulgar or suggestive language toward employees in your company.

■ An employee's friend or a customer visits the workplace and uses inappropriate language or gestures.

Preventing Harassment and Sexual Harassment

There are a number of steps that you as a manager can take to prevent harassment and sexual harassment. Two important steps are:

- Adopt a written policy regarding sexual harassment.

- Train employees and supervisors to identify and avoid inappropriate behaviors.

Adopt a Written Policy

Your organization's sexual harassment policy should clearly define inappropriate behaviors that can be construed as harassment or sexual harassment. At a minimum, the policy must include protection from harassment based on the categories defined in various federal laws. Some states require that other categories be added. Some organizations have voluntarily added categories such as sexual orientation, HIV, AIDS, and others to their policies.

Your policy must also include a procedure for employees to file complaints. The procedure should list specific people for the employee to contact to file a complaint. The employee's supervisor or manager or the company's human resources representatives and legal staff are possible contacts for employee complaints.

In most cases, employees will come forward to express their concerns if they believe their concerns will be heard and carefully considered. It is, therefore, important for the list of people who can be contacted to represent the gender and racial diversity of your organization.

There are a number of steps that you as a manager can take to prevent harassment and sexual harassment.

Your organization's sexual harassment policy should clearly define inappropriate behaviors that can be construed as harassment or sexual harassment.

3

> ## ✔ Self-Check
>
> When was the last time your organization offered training in the prevention of sexual harassment to employees? If it has been more than a year, it would be wise to schedule another session to remind people of the importance of avoiding inappropriate behaviors.
>
> How do new employees find out about your commitment to equal employment and preventing harassment and sexual harassment? Could the process be improved? How?

As with all management policies, the harassment policy is only effective if it is taken seriously and carefully enforced. As a supervisor, you must show that you support the policy through your actions and words:

- Avoid saying or doing anything that can be interpreted or misinterpreted as harassment or sexual harassment. Talk about your commitment to a harassment-free workplace.

- Be sympathetic and open to complaints and concerns raised by employees. Support open, objective investigations into complaints.

- Take appropriate disciplinary action against employees who are found to violate the policy.

Training to Avoid Inappropriate Behavior

Beyond creating a well-written policy and seeing that it is practiced and enforced, managers can be sure that everyone in the organization is trained to avoid a variety of inappropriate behaviors. A few of the many behaviors that should be discussed include inappropriate verbal contact, personal excuses, and inappropriate touching.

Inappropriate Verbal Contact

Inappropriate verbal contact occurs when one person says something (words or sounds) that offends another person. Most people use a three-part test to decide whether verbal communication is offensive:

- What was said?

- How was it said?

- Who said it?

Though most of us apply this test at the subconscious level, our answers determine whether we accept or reject another person's comments. For example, Matthew might say to Nicole:

"Good morning, Nicole. You look nice today."

Nicole might consider this a compliment because she knows Matthew very well, and she often hears him tell both men and women that they look nice. On the other hand, if David made the same comment to Nicole, she might consider it offensive because of the tone of his voice and the fact that she does not know him very well.

Supervisors should avoid making comments that can be misinterpreted. For example, if you want to compliment someone on how she or he looks, compliment the garment rather than the person:

"That's a lovely dress, Nicole. Is it new?"

If you compliment women, you should also regularly compliment men, and vice versa.

Inappropriate verbal contact occurs when one person says something (words or sounds) that offends another person.

3

Personal Excuses

Perhaps you have heard someone say something like, "I don't mean to call you sweetheart all the time, but it's just the way I am." Or maybe you have said, "I don't think she means anything by it. It's just the way she is."

These excuses are often warning signs of a complaint waiting to happen. You should listen for excuses like these (from yourself and others) and take steps to change the behaviors that cause them to be used.

Inappropriate Touching

There are many ways to touch another person. Most of them are inappropriate in a workplace environment. Some of the forms of touching most frequently complained about include:

The Search and Explore Touch—Whether intended or not, this is the most offensive of the inappropriate touching categories. It involves one person touching another to get a "cheap" feel. It may involve:
- Brushing up against the other person.
- Hugging or squeezing the other person as part of a greeting.
- Blatantly groping or touching the other person.

The Family Touch—Sometimes people touch other people because they come from a culture where touching is a normal way of interacting with others. When they bring this behavior into the workplace, they risk offending coworkers who do not understand, appreciate, or like being touched.

The Appreciation Touch—A third form of inappropriate touching is the appreciation touch. In this category, a supervisor might attempt to compliment an employee's work by reaching over and placing a hand on the thigh of the employee and saying, "Nice job. Thanks for your extra efforts."

No matter how well intended, a hand on the thigh is most likely unwelcome. A much better way to show appreciation would be to just make the comment or to make the comment and shake hands.

There are many ways to touch another person. Most of them are inappropriate in a workplace environment.

Avoid touching employees unless you are clear that your touch is welcome. Even if it is welcome to the person you are touching, your action may send a signal that you favor that person or others who allow you to touch them. A smile, a handshake, or a few kind words can be just as effective as a hug or a touch.

Stereotyping

Racial or sexual epithets, jokes, and stories stereotype people. When used in the workplace, they send a negative message about the role, level, or potential of people who are members of the targeted group. Pictures, posters, calendars, and cartoons have a similar effect. This is a difficult concept for some people:

"I don't know why we can't have a pinup in the shop. There aren't any women working out there."

The person making this statement misses the point. The picture would clearly send a message that women are not welcome in the shop as employees. It would also have a chilling effect on any women who might desire to seek an opportunity to work in the shop.

For Your Information

In a recent workshop, an employee objected to the restrictions that sexual harassment policies place on touching and other behavior in the workplace. I asked the employee how he would feel about those restrictions if a family member came home and complained about a coworker telling a dirty joke or touching her in an inappropriate manner. Without hesitation, the supervisor responded, "I'd go down and take care of the problem the next day!"

Many people carry a double standard of behavior into the workplace. In most cases, the standard we use for the treatment of family members is much higher than the standard we apply to coworkers. If the family standard were applied at work, we would see far fewer sexual harassment complaints.

3

Dating

Many companies have adopted policies that prevent or discourage supervisors from dating employees. When a supervisor dates an employee, there is considerable potential for a problem to develop. The supervisor must realize that he or she has direct or indirect power to influence the employment relationship or status of the employee. Even if the employee reports to someone else, the supervisor's comments can have an undue influence, positive or negative, on pay raises, performance ratings, and the morale of other employees in the work unit.

If the relationship experiences difficulties—or it ends—it can affect the morale, communication, and productivity of the entire work unit. Most important, the supervisor and the organization can be open to a charge that the relationship began or was prolonged out of concern for job security. The supervisor and the organization will then be forced to defend a quid pro quo sexual harassment claim.

Unless a conflict of interest exists, it would be very difficult to adopt a policy against coworkers dating. However, coworker dating can have a negative impact on productivity, communication, and morale. If members of your staff date, you must be sensitive to the impact of the relationship on the workplace environment. You must be prepared to step in and counsel or even discipline behavior that has a negative effect on the workplace environment.

Use Power in a Positive Way

In one organization, management trained employees and managers on expected behaviors. Seminars were held on harassment, sexual harassment, cultural and sexual diversity, interpersonal communication, how to use the grievance procedure, and other related topics. Not only were employees trained, but they were tested at the end of each session. People who scored low were referred for additional training or counseling. The positive use of management power established an environment where people of all types felt welcome and involved. Employees also reported that they were more productive than they had been in previous organizations.

Coworker dating can have a negative impact on productivity, communication, and morale.

✔ Self-Check

Appoint yourself as Training Manager for a moment. Write three training objectives for a workshop on harassment and sexual harassment. Focus on what you want the participants to be able to do when they complete the training.

As a result of attending this workshop, you will be able to:

1._____

2._____

3._____

3

Steps for the Effective Supervisor

Here are some suggestions to help you implement the information in this chapter. If you use them, they will help you avoid legal problems. They will also help you manage people in a way that shows you respect them and appreciate their efforts and contributions.

Step 1— Set a personal example for others with the language you use. Avoid slang and vulgar words and phrases. Call people by name. Avoid nicknames that may stereotype or label people. Avoid gender- and race-based labels.

Step 2— Avoid unnecessary touching. If you must touch a coworker, touch him or her only in a professional, businesslike manner. Shaking hands is a professional, businesslike way to touch.

Step 3— Take immediate steps to remove pictures, posters, cartoons, drawings, and other visual cues that may degrade or offend employees or visitors in your workplace.

Step 4— Do not date people with whom you work. Do not make suggestive remarks that might be interpreted as asking someone for a date or a sexual favor.

Step 5— Set high standards of behavior for employees in your department. Make it clear through your words and actions that you expect people to be treated with respect and dignity at work. Arrange for training on sexual harassment and diversity for employees in your department. Watch for problems or potential problems and address them early to keep them from becoming formal complaints.

Step 6— Take complaints seriously! If employees approach you with a concern about discrimination, harassment, or sexual harassment, take time to listen. Don't put them off. Get Human Resources and your manager involved as soon as possible. Follow up with employees to be sure they know you are concerned and are taking action.

Chapter Three Review

Now that you have read Chapter Three, use this space to review what you have learned so far. If you are not sure of an answer, just refer to the text. **Answers appear on page 113.**

1. **True or False?**
   All illegal harassment is based on sex.

2. The three most frequently discussed forms of workplace harassment are:

   a._____

   b._____

   c._____

3. Quid pro quo sexual harassment includes, but is not limited to:

   _____

   _____

   _____

4. Environmental sexual harassment includes, but is not limited to:

   _____

   _____

   _____

5. When it comes to discrimination, harassment, and sexual harassment, power can be used:

   a. In a negative way to:

   _____

   _____

   b. In a positive way to:

   _____

   _____

CHAPTER FOUR

Recruiting and Hiring

Chapter Objectives

After reading this chapter and completing the exercises, you should be able to:

 Plan a job-related employment interview.

 Take job-related interview notes.

 Make a complete, clear job offer.

Eric was preparing to conduct a round of interviews for a Computer Programmer position in his department. The vacancy came about because Danielle decided to start her own consulting practice. She was going to be missed not only for her excellent skills, but also because she got along well with all the other members of the team.

As he scanned through the résumés on his desk, Eric kept thinking about the importance of finding someone who would fit in with the group. Three of the four résumés gave him an idea of how the candidates would fit in with the group. One candidate, Nicole, belonged to the same sorority as Eric's sister. He could ask his sister to find out more about her. Another candidate, Chu, listed skiing, sailing, and club soccer as favorite activities. "That's good," he thought. "Sailing and soccer require working together with other people." The third candidate, Mo, listed chess, computer games, and wilderness hiking as hobbies. "This one is a loner," Eric thought. The fourth candidate did not list anything personal on the résumé. In addition, the name on the résumé was J. T. Winter. "Not a chance," thought Eric. "I can't even tell if this one is a guy or a gal."

Is Eric's thought process job-related? Is he discriminating either intentionally or unintentionally against these candidates?

A wide variety of employment laws work to ensure that qualified applicants are given a fair chance to compete for employment opportunities.

The Civil Rights Act, the Americans with Disabilities Act, and a variety of other employment laws affect how you recruit, hire, and promote employees. Access to a job and promotional opportunities are keys to success in our society. A wide variety of employment laws work to ensure that qualified applicants are given a fair chance to compete for employment opportunities.

Job-Relatedness

Job-relatedness is the one consistent theme in every law that affects recruiting and hiring. It is the most important concept for you to understand if you want to avoid discrimination. A *job-related* decision is based on objective criteria that are directly linked to doing the work that needs to be done. Your decisions should be based on objective information that allows you to reasonably predict whether a candidate will be successful on the job.

Everything Is a Test

One way to be sure you are making a job-related hiring decision is to view each step of the recruitment process as a test. When you ask someone to give you information to help you decide whether she or he is qualified for a job, you are testing that person. Like any test, your test should be fair; it should not have a disparate impact on a protected group.

The typical job applicant generally goes through a series of stages during the employment process, including:

- Reading an employment ad or job posting.
- Completing an employment application.
- Participating in an interview.
- Passing a background check.

Each of these stages can be seen as a test for the applicant. To avoid discrimination, you must be sure that each test is understandable, job-related, and graded in the same way for every candidate.

A *job-related* decision is based on objective criteria that are directly linked to doing the work that needs to be done.

4

Employment Ads

Printed employment ads and job postings describe job openings and invite interested persons to apply. Printed ads and postings also test an applicant's ability to see and understand printed material. Are these valid tests for all job situations?

The ability to see printed material is not necessary in all job situations. With the help of a talking computer, people who are sight-impaired can do a wide variety of office jobs. Even before the computer, sight-impaired people successfully performed jobs in many different occupations and businesses.

The ability to understand printed material is not necessary for every job opening. Many jobs, such as cutting grass, cleaning tables in a restaurant, or washing cars, do not require workers to be able to read complex sentences and paragraphs. A candidate with a mental disability might not be able to read an ad, but might be able to perform the job quite well.

💡 For Your Information

Placing an ad under a "Male" Help Wanted or "Female" Help Wanted column is discriminatory. In most cases, seeking a married candidate is also discriminatory.

The Americans with Disabilities Act prohibits discrimination in hiring based on physical and mental disabilities. To avoid discrimination, employers must offer alternative methods for applicants to learn about job openings. Large-print ads or postings can accommodate sight-impaired people. Organizations can also use a TDD machine, voice-recorded job postings, or other means to be sure that all qualified applicants are able to learn about openings.

✔ Self-Check

How does your organization advertise job openings?

What things could it do to make those job openings easier for people with disabilities to access?

_____

_____

_____

Employment Applications

Employment applications ask job applicants to describe their qualifications for a position. Printed applications also test an applicant's ability to write. Is this skill necessary for every job? How much personal information is really necessary for you to determine whether a candidate is qualified for a job?

As we discussed in the previous section on employment ads, every job does not require the ability to read. Likewise, all jobs do not require the ability to write. In some cases, it may be appropriate and necessary for you to help an applicant complete an employment application.

What information should your employment application request? Most applications ask for the applicant's name, address, education, and work experience. Even though this information may seem very basic, it should be requested only if it is job-related. For example, many applications still ask for the dates an applicant attended high school. You may need to know if the applicant graduated or earned a GED, but you do not need to know when that person attended school before you make a job offer. Since most people attend high school when they are teenagers, asking for attendance dates may allow you to estimate how old the candidate is. Under the Age Discrimination in Employment Act of 1967, you cannot consider the age of an applicant who is over 40 as a factor in your hiring decision. Age is rarely relevant to a job.

Some employment applications also ask for a driver's license number. Unless the job requires the applicant to drive, a driver's license number is not job-related. You may need to have applicants verify that they are indeed who they say they are. You can do this by asking an applicant to show you a valid form of identification after a job is offered.

4

For Your Information

In most cases, you should not ask to see a driver's license or other form of identification during an interview or at any time before you have offered the candidate a job. A driver's license (and other identification cards) often includes a birthdate and other information that is not job-related.

Interviews

An employment interview allows you to test an applicant's job qualifications more fully. What information do you need from an applicant in order to do this?

An employment interview should test an applicant's job qualifications, not the details of her or his personal life. Every question you ask must be job-related.

Many interviewers make the mistake of beginning an interview by discussing something personal or family-related. Personal and family issues are not job-related. Suppose an interviewer begins with:

"I'm glad you came for this interview. While you're getting settled, let me tell you about my weekend. We took our family to the beach. My kids had a really good time in the water."

Although no response is required, the applicant is somewhat obligated to respond with something about his or her family. If the applicant does not have a family, it may be awkward for him or her to respond. Not only is the interview off to a bad start, there is nothing job-related about whether or not a candidate has a family. The interviewer should start the interview with a statement such as:

"While you are getting settled, let me tell you a little bit about our company. We were founded by R.U. Camping in 1962. We manufacture motor homes for school playgrounds and parks."

The interviewer should go on to explain more about the company and share basic information about the job opening. A discussion like this is related to the company and the job.

The next step in an interview is to ask questions. Dr. Paul Green has developed a concept called *behavioral interviewing* [1] that can help you conduct a job-related interview. Three important features of a behavioral interview are:

- The interview is planned.

- The interview is based on the job.

- The interviewer asks the applicant to describe specific past experiences in order to illustrate her ability to perform the job.

When a candidate gives you specific information about what she has done in the past, you can reasonably assume that she will take a similar course of action in the future. An example of a behavioral interview question is:

"This job involves working with our customers. As you know, customers have many different needs and interests. Sometimes, they are unhappy with the services they receive. Tell me about a time when you were working with a customer who was unhappy with the service he or she had received. Why was the customer unhappy? What did the customer do? What did you do?"

A behavioral question encourages a candidate to give you specific information about a specific past experience. The information you gain will be more thorough than the answer you would receive to a hypothetical question about the future. This is true because the candidate is likely to repeat the behavior she describes in similar situations.

[1] For a more complete discussion of behavioral interviewing, see **Interviewing: More Than a Gut Feeling**, Richard S. Deems, Ph.D., American Media Publishing. American Media Incorporated has also produced a training video, **More Than a Gut Feeling II.**

4

Inappropriate Pre-employment Questions

In order to avoid discrimination, be careful when you ask interview questions in the following areas:

For Your Information

Many companies have adopted a team management concept. In some cases, the team actually does the interviewing and hiring of new employees. It is very important for every team member to understand the importance of planning and conducting job-related interviews.

In some team interviews, each team member is given an area to focus on during the interview. For example, one team member might ask a candidate about education. Another team member asks about work experience. A third team member explores specific technical skills.

Names—You need to know the name of a candidate to communicate with her. You may need to know whether she has ever gone by a different name to check references or educational accomplishments. You should not ask for a maiden name, because it tells you whether the applicant is married. In addition, asking for a maiden name usually only applies to women.

Age—The Age Discrimination in Employment Act of 1967 prohibits discrimination on the basis of age over 40. In most cases, you do not need to know the age of an applicant to make a job-related hiring decision. The Fair Labor Standards Act of 1938 (FLSA) and state laws place special requirements on hiring minors. You need to know if an applicant is under 18 to comply with the child labor provisions of the FLSA.

Birthplace, Citizenship—Under the Immigration Reform and Control Act of 1986, every new employee must provide proof that she is eligible to work in the United States. This is done by asking the candidate to complete an I-9 form. Since your only concern is whether the applicant is legally eligible to work in the United States, you should not ask questions about her birthplace or citizenship. Your application may include a statement that the applicant will be required to provide proof that she is eligible to work in the United States.

National Origin—It may be job-related for you to require an applicant to speak a second language. You can ask the candidate about her ability to speak other languages. You do not need to ask if that language is her "native tongue."

Gender, Marital Status, Family—Generally, you do not need to know or consider the gender, marital status, or family status of an applicant. If the applicant is a minor, you may need to know how to contact her parent(s) or guardian(s) in an emergency. If your organization has a policy that prohibits relatives from reporting to each other, state your policy and ask the candidate if she can comply with it. Questions about children, child care, pregnancy, and outside family interests are not job-related and should be avoided in an interview.

Physical Description, Photograph—With the possible exception of casting for movies or advertising, there is no legitimate reason to ask a candidate to describe her physical appearance.

✔ Self-Check

Look at your organization's employment application. Compare it to the list of issues discussed in this chapter. Does it need to be changed in any way? Discuss the changes you think are needed with your human resources professional or labor attorney.

Physical Condition, Disability—The Americans with Disabilities Act of 1990 (ADA) prohibits discrimination on the basis of a mental or physical disability. A disability can be a current disability such as a hearing aid, blindness, or Down's syndrome. Questions about disabilities are inappropriate.

When you ask a candidate a question about a job duty that requires physical or mental ability, you should frame your question to avoid discrimination under the ADA. Your question should be the same for apparently able-bodied candidates as it is for those with known disabilities. One way to ask such a question is:

"This job is in our warehouse. It involves moving boxed inventory on and off trucks. Normally, a forklift is used to move the inventory. Can you, with or without an accommodation, move inventory on and off trucks using a forklift?"

4

51

By adding the words "with or without an accommodation" to your question, you indicate to the candidate that you are willing to work with her to accommodate her disability as necessary.

Arrest, Criminal Record—In our society, people are considered innocent until proven guilty. You cannot ask about arrests. You can ask if the applicant has been convicted of a felony. You must give her an opportunity to explain the conviction. You must then consider whether the conviction is job-related and what effect it would have on the applicant's ability to perform the job.

Religion—The Civil Rights Act of 1964 prohibits discrimination on the basis of religion. In most cases, you do not need to know about an applicant's religious beliefs or affiliation before you make a job offer. In some cases, religious beliefs or affiliation may make it difficult or impossible for an individual to work a specific schedule. You must then decide if you can accommodate the religious practices or beliefs.

Organizations, Activities—There is a wide variety of gender, ethnic, religious, and other professional organizations. These organizations have given women and minorities leadership opportunities that they might not have received in other organizations. While you cannot ask about an applicant's membership in gender- or minority-based organizations, your application can give them the option, if they so desire, to discuss their participation and experience in such groups.

Emergency Notification—You can ask for the name of an emergency contact. You cannot ask for a family member to contact, because that information would likely tell you about the applicant's marital status or gender.

You should plan each interview carefully to avoid asking questions that are not job-related. You should write out job-related, behavioral interview questions and use the same basic questions for each candidate. You can ask follow-up questions to gain additional information. Organizing your questions in a format like this will help you remember your questions and document the applicant's answers.

When you conduct an interview, you should take notes to document what you learn from the candidate. Clear, well-written notes give you information to make job-related decisions. Your notes should reflect the actual information the candidate gives you. (A few notes are shown in the sample interview format below.) Your notes can show why you selected one candidate over another. Your best defense in a discrimination case is to show clear, job-related reasons why you picked one candidate over others. Your notes can be invaluable in making this point.

Applicant: Hector Gonzalez	**Date: November 16**
Position: Customer Service Rep.	**Interviewer:** NMD
Questions	**Answers**
1. This position involves answering questions from customers on the phone and completing paperwork. Please summarize your education and experience related to this position.	*Greeter at J-Mart two years. Took customer service class at community college. Volunteered on telephone teen-counseling service.*
2. Tell me about a time when you were helping a customer on the phone and you felt you were particularly effective. What did the customer say? What did you say? What was the outcome?	*Elderly customer confused about advertised product: directed customer to correct catalog section; stayed on phone with customer until questions answered; customer wrote complimentary letter.*

4

Reference Checks

It is very important for you to check references before you make an employment offer. At the same time, it can be very difficult to get information from previous employers. Let's look at each of these issues.

References provide an important means for you to verify a job applicant's qualifications.

References provide an important means for you to verify a job applicant's qualifications. If you hire an applicant without checking references, and that applicant does not have the qualifications he claimed, his inexperience could result in harm or injury to a third person. Your organization would then be open to charges of *negligent hiring*. Consider the following example:

A West Coast company is interested in an applicant who says that he worked for a similar company on the East Coast. Because of time-zone differences and a rush to hire someone, a reference check is not done. The applicant is offered the job. He accepts. A few months later, he starts a fight with a customer. The customer is injured. The customer's attorney checks the employee's references and finds that he did not work at the East Coast company, but was in prison for battery during the employment period he listed on the application. The customer claims the employee never should have been hired. If the employee had not been hired, the customer would not have been hurt.

Was the employer negligent?

A jury will very likely conclude that the employer negligently hired the employee. You must make a reasonable effort to confirm background information on every candidate you decide to hire. If you are unable to confirm information, you should ask the candidate to provide additional documentation.

Though checking references is important, it can also be difficult, because companies are concerned about being sued for defamation of character.

Ahmed has worked for a company for five years. He receives a performance review each year that rates him as "satisfactory." He decides to leave his job and go back to school for a year. When he starts applying for a new job, he gets several interviews. He feels good about the interviews, but he does not get a job offer. In frustration, he asks a friend to call his previous employer and ask for a reference check.

Ahmed's friend reports that the previous supervisor said, "Well, Ahmed was OK. We hate to lose good people, but in this case it wasn't a great loss. We had a question about some missing inventory. I would be careful. Don't tell him I said this, but we'd have to be pretty hard up to re-employ Ahmed here."

Clearly, there is a conflict between the "satisfactory" rating on Ahmed's past performance reviews and what his previous supervisor is telling potential employers. Either his supervisor was untruthful in his performance review or his supervisor is spreading untruthful information about him in the community. Either way, Ahmed is being treated unfairly.

✔ Self-Check

Do you know how your organization handles reference checks? Ask your human resources professional to explain your policy or practice.

Companies have learned to avoid this unnecessary liability by confirming only factual information in a reference check. As a result, when you call for a reference, the person you talk to will normally verify only information about a current or former employee's job title and length of employment. You should also attempt to verify other factual information the applicant provides on the employment application.

You must follow your company's policy when you check references. In most cases, the company policy is that all references be done by Human Resources. This helps ensure that they are done consistently and legally. Give your human resources representative a list of job-related information that you want her to attempt to get in a reference check, and carefully consider the job-related information she provides to you. You should wait until the reference check is complete before you make a final decision about a candidate.

Medical Testing

Under the Americans with Disabilities Act, you may not discriminate against an applicant because of a mental or physical condition. Therefore, if you ask an applicant to take a medical examination before you make a job offer, you will be obtaining information that could tell you if the applicant has a disability. If you have that information, it may influence your decision to hire or not hire the applicant. Using the information could be considered discrimination.

In order to avoid disability discrimination, you must wait to ask an applicant to take a medical exam until after you make an employment offer. Under the ADA, the medical exam must be based on the essential job functions. Therefore, the medical examiner must have information about the essential functions the employee will be performing. If the medical exam does reveal a disability, you will need to analyze the situation to determine whether you can make a reasonable accommodation to allow the otherwise qualified employee to do the job.

If you require a medical exam, you must require all of the people who receive a job offer for that type of job to take it. If only some of the successful candidates are asked to take the exam, it may appear that they have been identified as having a perceived disability.

If you require a medical exam, you must require all of the people who receive a job offer for that type of job to take it.

Pre-employment Drug Testing

Many companies conduct pre-employment drug tests. (We will discuss postemployment drug testing later.) Many larger retail stores, for example, now display prominent signs that say something to the effect of "We test all applicants for illegal drugs. If you use drugs, don't apply."

Though drug testing is controversial, the courts have generally permitted it for pre-employment screening. Generally, the reasoning is that an applicant has a choice about whether or not she wants to apply for a job. Because the choice is voluntary, the applicant does not have to submit to it. Therefore, if the applicant is told about the test in advance, pre-employment drug testing is generally permissible. Because state laws vary on this subject, you should check with human resources before you discuss drug testing with applicants.

In some cases, federal law may require drug testing. For example, Department of Transportation and Department of Defense regulations require drug testing for certain employees.

The Employment Offer

When you offer an applicant a job, you are entering into an agreement with him or her. It is important for that agreement to be clear and specific. It is also important for you to understand that you must live up to the terms of your job offer. Many companies require that job offers be made in writing to reduce the possibility of confusion about salary, benefits, and other terms and conditions of employment.

Whether you write your job offer or make it in person or over the phone, you must be careful to avoid making an implied contract between you and the applicant. An *implied contract* can be created when you make a statement or take an action that sets up an expectation for the applicant. For example, let's say that a supervisor makes a job offer to an applicant on the phone. At the end of the conversation, the supervisor says:

"I really hope you decide to come to work for us. We have a great group that gets along really well. I know you'll fit in. I know you'll be with us for a long time."

Is the supervisor making an implied contract?

Though drug testing is controversial, the courts have generally permitted it for pre-employment screening.

4

Whether you write your job offer or make it in person or over the phone, you must be careful to avoid making an *implied contract* between you and the applicant.

The supervisor's last statement, *"I know you'll be with us for a long time,"* could be interpreted as an implied contract. If the employee does not work out and is released during her *introductory period,* she may have a case for coming back to say that a promise of long-term employment was broken. The supervisor should have said something like:

"I really hope you decide to come to work for us. Your job will involve writing technical manuals for our computer software. Like all of our employees, you will be an at-will employee. This means that either you or the company may end the employment relationship at any time for any reason."

While you may at first feel that this language is somewhat cold and stark, it is an honest explanation of the terms under which the applicant is being asked to join the company. Unless you are willing to live up to unclear promises, you must be very careful to explain the employment relationship in clear, specific terms.

✔ Self-Check

In one case, a company wrote a letter to an applicant that said:

"During your first year, your salary will be $70,000. During your second year, it will increase to $80,000. In your third year, your salary will be $90,000 plus bonuses."

The employee was released during the first 90 days of employment. The employee sued, claiming that the letter created a three-year employment agreement. Do you agree? (The jury agreed and awarded the employee salary and damages for the remaining term of the contract.)

Initial Employment

Until the 1970s, the first three months of employment were commonly referred to as the *probation period.* The probation period grew out of the union movement. When unions first began organizing workers, they insisted that they be allowed to represent employees from their first day of employment. Management, however, wanted time to evaluate new employees to see if they had hired the right person for the job. The probation period was created to meet the needs of both management and the unions. It gave management time to evaluate the employee, but allowed the union to protect the employee after the probation period.

Over time, nonunion companies also adopted the probation-period concept. In fact, in many companies, the employee handbook included language such as:

"You will serve a 90-day probationary period. During this time, your supervisor will decide if you are properly suited for the job. If you complete the probation period, you will become a permanent employee."

In the 1970s, employees began to challenge such statements. They argued that, under this language, an employer had to make a decision about an employee's success during the first 90 days of employment. They also argued that after the 90-day probation period had passed, the employer could not terminate the employee, because there was an implied contract for permanent (i.e., never-ending) employment.

Employers argued that despite the language in the handbook, all employees were *at-will,* and the employer could terminate employment at any time. They argued that at-will employment took precedence over any language in the employee handbook.

4

Many courts sided with employees in these cases because the language in the employee handbook established a higher level of job security for the employee. As a result, nonunion employers began to drop their use of the term *probation period.* In some cases, they adopted a term such as *introductory period* or *training period.* In other cases, companies chose to tell new employees they would be at-will from their first day of employment until their employment ended either by their own choice or by the choice of the company.

In companies where the introductory or training period is used, it is frequently described in terms such as:

"Your employment with the company is at-will. This means that you or the company may terminate your employment at any time for any reason. Only the President can change your at-will status. Any such change must be made in writing and signed by the President. We call your initial period of employment an introductory period. During this time, your supervisor will carefully observe and evaluate your work to determine if you are properly qualified to perform your job according to our performance expectations. Your supervisor will also evaluate your ability to learn your new job."

Notice that unlike the first example, there is no specific period of time for the introductory period described in this example. Secondly, there is no promise of any change in employment after the introductory period is completed.

When you make a job offer, you need to be sure that you understand your company's policy concerning the initial employment period.

When you make a job offer, you need to be sure that you understand your company's policy concerning the initial employment period. You need to be sure that you explain it clearly to potential employees. You also need to be sure you do not alter your company's policy by making an implied contract by saying something like, *"We have an introductory period, but no one* ever *pays attention to it."*

✔ Self-Check

How does your organization treat the initial employment period. What is it called? How long does it last? How is it explained in your employee handbook? How do you explain it during a job offer?

_____

_____

_____

_____

4

Steps for the Effective Supervisor

Here are some suggestions to help you implement the information in this chapter. If you use them, they will help you avoid legal problems. They will also help you manage people in a way that shows you respect them and appreciate their efforts and contributions.

Step 1— Before you begin the process of filling a vacant position, sit down and write out the job duties you will want the new employee to perform. Don't depend on a job description. List the tasks you expect the person to do (e.g., typing, assembling, etc.). Define the results you expect them to produce (e.g., error-free software programming)

Step 2— Work with your human resources representative to define the qualifications a person will need to have to do the job successfully. Define qualifications related to abilities, knowledge, education, experience, and licenses (use only the categories that apply to the job).

Step 3— Plan your interviews. Have a list of job-related questions that you will ask every candidate. Use behavioral questions that give you reliable information about past performance to help you predict future performance. Take clear, job-related, factual notes during the interview.

Step 4— Work with your human resources representative to conduct a job-related reference check on each candidate. Make sure notes are kept on the information provided by the reference sources.

Step 5— Give frequent, honest, and objective feedback to new employees.

Chapter Four Review

Now that you have read Chapter Four, use this space to review what you have learned so far. If you are not sure of an answer, just refer to the text. **Answers appear on page 113.**

1. **True or False?**
   Everything you do in a recruitment is a test.

2. All employment tests must be:

   _____

3. Behavioral interviewing means: (choose one)
   a. Asking the candidate to stand up and demonstrate a behavior while you watch.

   b. Asking job-related questions that encourage the employee to talk about specific past experiences to help you predict his future performance.

   c. Role-playing a job-related scenario with a candidate.

4. The Age Discrimination in Employment Act prohibits discrimination in employment of persons over the age of:_____

5. Reference checks are: (choose one)

   a. A waste of time because no one will give you information anymore.

   b. Easy to do because everyone understands how important they are.

   c. Essential to make sure that the candidate has given you accurate information about work experience and education.

   d. Important to do to avoid negligent hiring.

   e. Answers b and d.

   f. Answers c and d.

CHAPTER FIVE

At-Will, Performance, and Discipline

Chapter Objectives

After reading this chapter and completing the exercises, you should be able to:

- ☑ Explain the concept of at-will employment.

- ☑ List three objective reasons for terminating an employee.

- ☑ Plan a job-related performance review.

- ☑ Explain the steps of progressive discipline.

Rebecca looked at Bob's personnel file and shook her head. Despite a good deal of training and coaching, Bob simply was unable to perform his job at company standards. He was such a nice person, though, she hated to fire him. "I could tell him that we're downsizing and his position is being eliminated," she thought. "Then it will seem more like a layoff than a firing. I wonder if that's legal?"

Managing performance is one of your most important supervisory responsibilities. You must establish performance goals and standards for employees and provide timely feedback to them on their job performance. If an employee does not perform the job properly, or if he violates a company rule, it is your responsibility to address the problem in a timely manner. Along the way, you must take into consideration a variety of legal principles designed to protect the employee from unfair treatment.

At-Will Employment

At-will employment is a legal concept that creates four basic employment rights:

- An employer may offer employment to a job candidate at the employer's will (within the constraints of various antidiscrimination statutes).

- A job candidate may accept or reject a job offer at his will.

- An employee may terminate his employment at his will, at any time, for any reason.

- An employer may terminate an employee, at any time, for any reason, or for no reason, so long as it is not an illegal reason.

In short, at-will employment gives you the right to hire and fire employees. However, it is not an unfettered right. You must act responsibly and within the limits of the law. At-will employment is like a driver's license. Your driver's license gives you the right to drive an automobile. It does not give you the right to speed or drive recklessly in a way that causes harm to others. In the same way, when you hire, discipline, or terminate an employee, you must make your decision in a nondiscriminatory and fair manner.

You should never terminate an employee unless you have an objective reason for your action.

5

Objective Reasons for Termination

Unless you want to be named in a lawsuit that you will very likely lose, you should never terminate an employee without an objective reason for your action. An objective reason is based on facts that can be shown to be true with documentation or other proof. There are three objective reasons for terminating an employee:

- **Reduction in force**

- **Violation of company rules**

- **Inability or failure to perform**

Reduction in Force

Business needs and conditions change over time. Sometimes that change makes it necessary to reduce the size of the workforce. In other words, people are asked to give up their jobs through no fault of their own. A *reduction in force* may be based on:

- A change in technology that eliminates the need for the employee's position or requires a new set of skills that the employee does not possess and cannot obtain in a reasonable period of time.

- The elimination of a position for organizational, financial, or other legitimate business reasons. The decision to combine the duties of one or more positions to reduce overhead or eliminate duplication of effort.

A reduction in force must be supported by:

- Documentation that explains objective business reasons (e.g., technology, financial, etc.) for eliminating positions.

- Documentation that shows objective criteria for selecting employees (e.g., seniority, performance review ratings, etc.) to be included in the reduction in force.

✔ Self-Check

What is the layoff policy for your organization? What criteria would be used to select people for a layoff? For recall?

If a reduction in force cannot be supported by objective reasons, it is very likely a *subterfuge termination*. A subterfuge termination occurs when an employee is told that he is being laid off when he is actually being terminated for poor performance. The courts are full of subterfuge termination lawsuits. These cases are frequently lost by the employer because juries often assume a subterfuge was used to hide discrimination based on a protected class.

In addition to ensuring that a layoff is based on objective reasons, employers must also comply with the federal Worker Adjustment and Retraining Notification Act (WARN). WARN requires employers with more than 100 employees to give 60 days notice, under certain conditions, before laying off or terminating 50 or more employees.

Your potential liability does not end with a reduction in force. If employees are called back or rehired, you must follow your policy and use objective criteria to decide who is re-employed. For example, if your policy says that employees will be rehired based on seniority, you must follow it. If you make exceptions, you may create adverse impact or adverse treatment discrimination for one or more employees. If a former employee applies to work for the company at a later time, you must consider her previous experience objectively. For example, if her personnel file reflects that she was a satisfactory employee, you cannot now reject her re-employment because she did not work up to standards.

If employees are called back or rehired, you must follow your policy and use objective criteria to decide who is re-employed.

5

Violation of Company Rules

Another objective reason for terminating an employee is a violation of a company rule or policy. Depending on the actual circumstances, a single violation may be sufficient to terminate an employee. For example, if an employee brings a gun to work in violation of a company policy, he would, following an objective investigation of the facts, likely be terminated immediately. In other cases, it may be necessary to first counsel and discipline the employee before termination, as when dealing with tardiness or absenteeism.

✔ Self-Check

Can you identify any rules in your organization that would lead to immediate termination if violated?

_____

_____

_____

_____

Inability or Failure to Perform

The third objective reason for terminating an employee is inability or failure to perform. You must be able to support your contention that the employee is failing to meet performance standards with objective reasons. Your reasons must be supported by documentation such as performance reviews and disciplinary action letters you have discussed with the employee and placed in her personnel file.

At-Will Employment Versus Objective Reasons for Termination

In theory, the concept of at-will employment gives you the right to terminate an employee without a reason. In practice, however, you must carefully consider and document your reasons for terminating an employee. For example, if an employee claims he was terminated for a discriminatory reason, you will have to explain why you did not discriminate. It is very difficult to prove what you did not do. On the other hand, if you have counseled the employee about the problem and documented your efforts, you will be able to show that you used valid objective reasons to try to help the employee succeed before you made a decision to terminate him.

If an employee is performing poorly, you must be able to show that:

■ He knew what was expected of him.

■ You notified the employee of your concern in a timely manner.

■ You explained what the employee needed to do to correct the problem.

■ You explained to the employee that failure to correct the problem would result in disciplinary action up to and including termination.

5

Performance Reviews

Most employers give employees performance reviews. Interestingly, the law does not specifically require performance reviews. However, when they are given, they must be job-related, timely, and objective.

Your performance review should confirm and reinforce performance feedback you have given during the review period. It should not contain any surprises. Keep notes of your conversations about performance as well as copies of work that show effective and problem performance. When you write a performance review, refer to these notes and work samples. The review should summarize these conversations and provide your overall assessment of the employee's contributions.

The purpose of a performance review is to have a positive impact on future performance. You should write the review to help the employee understand how you want him to perform in the future. Your goal for the employee's future performance can be to continue good performance, to improve in areas that are below company standards, or to adapt to new job responsibilities.

Progressive Discipline

Unfortunately, you will encounter employees whose performance is not up to company standards. *Progressive discipline* places the employee on notice that there is a problem and that something must be done to correct it. Progressive discipline is usually required by a union contract and is normally used for public employees. In private sector, nonunion companies, the employer can decide whether to use progressive discipline. There are six basic steps in progressive discipline.[2]

> 1. **Training**
>
> 2. **Counseling**
>
> 3. **Oral Warning**
>
> 4. **Written Warning**
>
> 5. **Last-Step Option**
>
> 6. **Termination**

[2] For information on how to use progressive discipline, see **Documenting Discipline**, Mike Deblieux, American Media Publishing, 1995.

The purpose of a performance review is to have a positive impact on future performance.

Progressive discipline **places the employee on notice that there is a problem and that something must be done to correct it.**

The first two steps in progressive discipline carry no threat to the employee's job; the final four carry progressively more serious consequences leading up to termination, as illustrated in Figure 1.

Figure 1

```
                                                    ┌──────────────┐
                                                    │ Termination  │
                                        ┌───────────┴──────┐       │
                                        │ Last-Step Option │       │
                          ┌─────────────┴────────┐         │       │
                          │ Written Warning      │         │       │
            ┌─────────────┴────────┐             │         │       │
            │ Oral Warning         │             │         │       │
            └──────────────────────┘             │         │       │
```

CONSEQUENCE LINE

Training	Counseling

Progressive discipline is designed to create an opportunity for an employee with a performance problem to succeed. You cannot make an employee solve a performance problem; you can only create an opportunity for that employee to improve. When an employee has a performance problem, it is your job to:

■ Identify and explain the problem to the employee.

■ Define what needs to be done to correct it.

■ Offer the employee help to improve performance.

■ Communicate the potential consequence of the employee's failure to improve performance.

5

✔ Self-Check

An employee represents an investment of company resources. Your organization spends a significant amount of money to recruit employees. It also spends money to train them, purchase equipment for them, and help them acclimate to organizational culture. Try to determine how much it costs to recruit and train an employee in your organization.

How much of an investment would you lose by firing an employee?

If the employee is unsuccessful below the consequence line, you must take the informal action of training or counseling him. If the employee continues to be unsuccessful, you must cross the consequence line and take formal action up to and including termination. When you use the steps above the line, you must tell the employee, in writing, that his job is in jeopardy.

If an employee violates a rule or performs poorly, it is your responsibility as a supervisor to address the problem in a timely, fair, and consistent manner. If you use progressive discipline, you can show that the employee received training and was counseled or given help before you took disciplinary action. You will be able to document that you gave the employee increasingly serious warnings and an opportunity to correct the problem.

To protect yourself and your organization from liability, you must do two things at each step of the progressive discipline process:

Meet with the employee. Conduct a thorough investigation to be sure you understand the problem and give the employee a chance to explain his side of the story. If you decide that progressive discipline is necessary, carefully outline what you will say to the employee. You must be calm, rational, and clear. Everything you say must be designed to create an opportunity for the employee to be successful.

💡 For Your Information

An acronym to remember when you have to document employee discipline is FOSA+. It stands for Facts (Who, What, When, Where, Why), Objectives (explaining what must be done to correct the problem), Solutions (helping the employee by offering tips or suggestions), and Actions (explaining the consequences of not meeting the objectives). The + stands for your overall approach to the employee. It must be based on a commitment to help the employee succeed. FOSA+ is an agenda for meeting with an employee. It is also an outline for a discipline memo.

Document your actions. When you train (in a classroom or on the job), keep a record of when the training was done and what was covered. When you counsel an employee, make a note of what was said and what was supposed to take place as a result of the counseling. These should not be secret notes. The employee should know you are keeping them and what they say.

When you give an employee an oral warning, a written warning, or a last-step option, write a memo. Your memo should define the problem, explain what led up to the situation, and describe what needs to be done to correct it. It should offer the employee some ideas or assistance for correcting the problem, and it should communicate to the employee that failure to correct the problem will result in further discipline up to and including termination. If you terminate an employee, you should write a memo explaining the problems that led up to the termination, your suggestions to correct the problem, and the employee's failure to comply.

Other Employment Principles

Obviously, it is inappropriate to discipline or terminate an employee because of race, sex, religion, national origin, color, disability, age, and other unlawful reasons. However, in addition to these reasons, there are some other principles that you must consider before making a decision to discipline or terminate an employee. Three of the principles most often violated are:

- **Good faith and fair dealing**

- **Public policy**

- **Express contracts**

Good Faith and Fair Dealing

When you accept a job, you expect to have an open, honest relationship with your employer. The legal principle for this expectation is known as the *implied covenant of good faith and fair dealing*. This promise is implied by law in every contract.

If you hold a job over a period of time, you will probably come to feel that you have made a significant investment in the job. You will feel secure in your job and make life decisions such as buying a car or a house on the assumption that the job will continue. Your employer has created an implied contract of termination only for good cause.

If your job is in jeopardy, you expect your employer to give you advance notice and provide good reasons for the decision. If those reasons are not forthcoming, you will probably feel that you have been treated unfairly.

An employee worked for a company for more than 30 years. One day, the president called him into the office and told him that he was being terminated. When the employee asked for a reason for the termination, the president said, "You'll have to look in your heart for the answer to that question."

Was the employee treated unfairly?

The jury found that the employee was entitled to a more substantial explanation and that the implied contract of good faith and fair dealing and termination only for good cause had been breached. The employer was forced to pay a substantial amount to the former employee.

Public Policy

A public policy is a legal principle that places the needs and rights of the general public ahead of the rights of a company.

You cannot terminate an employee in *violation of a public policy*. A public policy is a legal principle that places the needs and rights of the general public ahead of the rights of a company.

A truck driver was terminated because he frequently complained about the brakes on his truck. The driver filed a complaint about the brakes with the highway patrol. The highway patrol inspected the brakes on the company's trucks and found several of them to be unsafe.

The driver took his employer to court, where he argued that, despite his supervisors' claims, he was not just a disruptive employee, but rather an employee who was trying to protect the general public from unsafe trucks on the highway.

Was the company justified in firing the driver?

The jury found that the company and the supervisor violated a public policy by firing the employee.

Express Contracts

Once you enter into an agreement with an employee, you must honor that agreement. Your agreements can be in writing or oral. If terminating an employee breaches an express contract, the company will be held liable for its actions.

Your employee handbook promises that you will use progressive discipline before you terminate an employee. A particular employee is creating a morale problem in your department by her excessive absenteeism and tardiness.

Must you use progressive discipline when dealing with this employee?

You must honor your express contract and use progressive discipline.

Take Care in Decision Making

As we have seen, at-will employment does not give supervisors the right to fire employees at the drop of a hat. Maintaining good performance, managing discipline, and making a termination all require well-reasoned, well-documented decisions. As you approach employment situations in your department, remember that the most important part of your job as a supervisor is to help your organization use its most valuable resource—people—effectively.

Steps for the Effective Supervisor

Here are some suggestions to help you implement the information in this chapter. If you use them, they will help you avoid legal problems. They will also help you manage people in a way that shows you respect them and appreciate their efforts and contributions.

Step 1— Find out if your organization has a policy on layoffs or reductions in force. Read it carefully. Ask questions about how it is used. When employees ask you questions about layoffs, refer them to the policy. Be sure that any comments you make are supported by the policy.

Step 2— Address performance and rule-violation problems each time they occur. Do not wait in the hope that the problem will go away. Use FOSA+ to address the problem. Always give the employee an opportunity to explain his or her side of the story before you decide on a course of action. Remember, unless the problem warrants immediate termination, it is your job to create an opportunity for the employee to be successful. It is up to the employee to decide if he or she is going to take advantage of the opportunity.

Step 3— Write and present performance reviews before they are actually due. Use specific examples to show the employee how you view her or his performance. Write the review to motivate the employee toward a future performance goal.

Step 4— Plan on keeping any promises you make to an employee. Be sure you can follow through before you tell an employee she will be promoted. Make sure you have approval before you make a job offer. In other words, don't make promises you can't keep.

Chapter Five Review

Now that you have read Chapter Five, use this space to review what you have learned so far. If you are not sure of an answer, just refer to the text. **Answers appear on page 114.**

1. *At-will employment* means that an employer may terminate an employee:

   _____

   _____

   _____

2. The three objective reasons for terminating an employee are:

   _____

   _____

   _____

3. **True or False?**
   An express contract must be in writing.

4. The most important thing a supervisor needs to understand about progressive discipline is that (choose one):

   a. He must follow each step in order each time an employee does something wrong.

   b. He must document each step of progressive discipline.

   c. It creates an opportunity for the employee to be successful.

   d. He can't expect to win every case.

5

Compensation

Chapter Objectives

After reading this chapter and completing the exercises, you should be able to:

 Explain the concept of equal pay for equal work.

 List the major provisions of the Fair Labor Standards Act.

☑ Discuss basic principles of overtime pay under the Fair Labor Standards Act of 1938.

Angel was frustrated. After she graduated from college, her first job as a marketing specialist didn't pay well, but she'd learned a lot. Now she had an offer for a new job. The position was perfect. The firm had the newest technology, and she would be a team leader. Her work would take her to places like Paris and Rio de Janeiro, and the company encouraged side trips. Best of all, her old friend Garret had just joined the firm. They would be able to collaborate again as they had in college.

There was just one problem with this job offer. The company wanted to give her a 10 percent increase over her salary at her previous firm. When she asked Garret what he got when he joined the firm, he told her that he also received a 10 percent increase over his previous salary. But Garret had gone to work for a larger firm when he graduated from college and had started at a higher salary than Angel. Now they would be doing the same job at the same firm, and Garret would make more than $1,000 more each month than Angel. Somehow, it didn't seem fair.

When you decide how much to pay an employee, you must consider several legal issues including:

■ Compensating employees on the basis of equal pay for equal work.

■ Offering at least the minimum wage.

■ Classifying the job as *exempt* or *nonexempt* for overtime.

Equal Pay for Equal Work

The Equal Pay Act of 1963 requires covered employers to pay men and women similar compensation when they are performing work that is substantially similar in skill, effort, and responsibility when the work is performed under similar working conditions in the same facility. (While the Equal Pay Act prohibits discrimination based only on gender, remember that the Civil Rights Act and other laws prohibit discrimination in all personnel practices, including pay based on race, religion, national origin, color, and other protected categories.)

One of the best ways to avoid pay discrimination is to have a pay plan that is based on:

- The actual work performed by employees.

- Pay ranges or pay grade.

- Consistent procedures for merit increases.

You can picture a pay plan by stacking boxes on top of each other:

```
                                 ┌─────────────────────┐
                                 │  Senior Technician  │
                   ┌─────────────┤                     │
                   │ Technician II│                    │
   ┌───────────────┤             ├─────────────────────┘
   │  Technician I  │            │
   │               ├─────────────┘
   └────────────────┘
```

Imagine that the job duties for each job title fit within the borders of the box. People performing those duties, regardless of their gender and other protected categories, should receive similar pay. In order for this system to work, three things must happen:

- The size and shape of the boxes must be based on actual work performed.

- The boxes must be given a value. The value can be an hourly pay rate, a salary, or a pay range.

6

79

All employees performing similar work must be paid according to the established value. The people performing the work must be paid based on the work they are performing. Let's look at an example:

Stephanie is a Technician I. She came to the company with no work experience, but excellent training and education. She is the only female technician. Karl is a Technician II. He has learned his skills on the job over a period of several years. He has little formal education. Stephanie has learned her new job quickly. In fact, when he will let her, Stephanie helps Karl solve some of his more difficult technical problems. Because she is good, she has been given increasingly more difficult assignments. In fact, everyone knows she has been performing Tech II work for at least six months. When Stephanie asks for a promotion to Technician II, she is told, "Stephanie, we would love to give you a promotion, but you haven't been here long enough. Karl and the other Tech IIs wouldn't like it if we paid you what we are paying them. Besides, you're single. They have families to feed."

Is Stephanie being treated fairly?

Clearly, Stephanie is not being paid on the basis of equal pay for equal work. The work she is performing is similar to the work Karl and others are performing. It requires similar skill, effort, and responsibility and is performed under similar working conditions. Her work should have the same value as the work performed by other Technician IIs. Stephanie's marital status and whether or not she has a family have nothing to do with the value of the work she is performing.

Notice that we have avoided saying identical pay in this discussion. The Equal Pay Act does not necessarily require identical pay for similar work. It does require similar pay for similar work. For example, a bona fide seniority plan might cause two employees doing similar work to be paid differently. Consider what might happen if Stephanie was promoted to Tech II status.

The Equal Pay Act does not necessarily require identical pay for similar work. It does require similar pay for similar work.

Stephanie and Karl are covered by a union contract. They are both paid $9 per hour. The union contract provides an extra $0.25 per hour for each year of service over ten years. Karl has been with the company for 14 years. As a result, he is actually paid $10 per hour. Under this scenario, Stephanie and Karl are paid "equally" as defined by the Equal Pay Act.

The same thing would be true if Stephanie and Karl were at different points in an established pay range.

The pay range for Technician II is $7.65 to $10.35 per hour. Stephanie makes $7.65 because she is new to the level of Tech II. Karl has progressed through the pay range over the years and has reached the top pay of $10.35. They are being paid "equally" because Stephanie has the potential to move through the pay range over time, just as Karl did.

Your company should have an established pay plan that is updated on a regular basis. You should learn about the plan and how it affects employees that report to you. You should pay employees within the guidelines established by your company's pay plan and without regard to protected categories. If an employee's job duties change significantly, you should recommend that Human Resources *reclassify* the employee's position to a more appropriate level.

Minimum Wage

The Fair Labor Standards Act of 1938 (FLSA) establishes the minimum wage. It requires you to pay nonexempt employees overtime and places restrictions on the employment of minors. It also requires you to pay men and women similar pay for similar work under similar circumstances. (The Equal Pay Act, which we have already discussed, was a 1964 amendment to the Fair Labor Standards Act.) FLSA is enforced by the Department of Labor.

Congress sets the minimum wage through amendments to the FLSA. It is periodically reviewed and changed. You must pay the minimum wage for all work performed by employees covered by the FLSA. Occasionally a state law will set a higher minimum wage than the one set by the FLSA. When the state law requires a higher amount, you must pay employees working in that state the higher rate.

Congress sets the minimum wage through amendments to the FLSA. It is periodically reviewed and changed.

Overtime Rate

The FLSA requires *nonexempt employees* to be paid one and one-half times their regular rate of pay for all hours worked over 40 hours in a workweek. A nonexempt employee may not give up her right to be paid overtime. (Some state laws require overtime after eight hours in a day.) An *exempt employee* is not eligible for overtime pay.

Exempt and Nonexempt Employees

The FLSA assumes that all employees are nonexempt (i.e., eligible for overtime) unless they fit into an exempt category (i.e., not covered by the FLSA's overtime provisions). An exemption is not determined by an employee's job title. An employee's actual job duties determine whether or not she is exempt. The employee must spend a substantial amount of time performing the exempt duties to qualify for the exemption. In addition, an employee is not automatically exempt just because she earns a salary.

FLSA includes a variety of exemptions. The three most frequently applied exemptions are:[3]

- executive
- administrative
- professional

An **exempt executive** is an employee whose primary duty is management of the business. In this case, management includes:

- Interviewing, selecting, and training employees.
- Directing and evaluating the work of employees.
- Handling complaints and grievances.
- Disciplining employees.
- Planning and assigning work.
- Determining how the work will be done.

An executive employee must supervise two or more employees on a regular basis. In addition, an executive employee must customarily and regularly make decisions or offer recommendations that are carefully considered.

[3] Our discussion of these exemptions is intended to give you an overview of each category. You should consult your human resources or legal advisor before deciding if a specific position is exempt or nonexempt.

The Fair Labor Standards Act assumes that all employees are eligible for overtime pay unless they fit into an exempt category.

An **exempt administrative** employee performs office or nonmanual work related to management policies or general business operations. This work normally involves:

- Using discretion and independent judgment to help an owner, executive, or administrative employee.
- Specialized or technical work assignments that are completed under general supervision.

Examples of administrative work include:

- Advising management on business operations.
- Planning substantial business activities.
- Negotiating on behalf of the business.
- Representing the business.
- Making significant purchasing decisions.

An **exempt professional** employee must be involved in work that is performed as a result of knowledge or skill gained through a long course of study (e.g., CPA, attorney, scientist) or artistic pursuit (e.g., music, writing, theater, graphic arts). The work performed by a professional employee must involve the use of discretion and independent judgment. The work must be predominantly intellectual and varied (e.g., not standardized).

✔ Self-Check

Make a list of exempt positions in your department. Based on the brief explanation of exemptions in this chapter, which exemption do you think applies to each position?

Exemption   Position Title

There are other exemptions for recreational employees, hospital and nursing home employees, agricultural employees, outside salespeople, and others. Before deciding if an individual position is exempt or nonexempt, you should consult with an experienced human resources professional or labor attorney to be sure you have considered all the available exemptions and criteria.

6

Time Worked

Under the FLSA, a nonexempt employee must be paid at least the minimum wage for all hours of work, whether the work is authorized or not. As a result, it is important to establish and enforce starting and quitting times for nonexempt employees. It is also important to establish and enforce meal-period times for nonexempt employees. If a nonexempt employee begins work early, works through her assigned lunch period, or works beyond the scheduled work day, she must be paid for the hours worked, even if the work hours were not authorized. (While you must pay the employee, you should also discipline her for violating a company rule against working unauthorized hours.)

The Workweek

When a nonexempt employee works more than 40 hours in a *workweek*, you must pay her one and one-half times her regular rate of pay for all hours of work over 40 hours. The FLSA defines the workweek as a seven-day period. The FLSA assumes the workweek is a seven-day period that starts at 12 a.m. Sunday and ends at 12 a.m. the following Sunday unless the employer establishes, in writing, a different seven-day period.

Regular Rate of Pay

An employee's *regular rate of pay* includes all the pay received for work performed during a seven-day period. For example, shift premiums, performance bonuses, annual performance bonuses, hazardous-duty pay, and other similar pay is included in the regular rate of pay. The regular rate of pay is calculated by dividing the employee's total compensation by the total number of hours worked in the workweek.

Hue makes $10 an hour. She works 48 hours in a seven-day period. She's paid $400 ($10 x 40) for the first 40 hours of work. She is paid time and one-half for the eight hours of overtime ($10 x 1.5 = $15). Her overtime pay is $120 ($15 x 8 = $120). She is paid $520 ($400 + $120 = $520) for the week.

Let's assume that during the workweek, Hue is paid $1 an hour for shift differential. She also receives $1.25 for serving as a lead worker. She works a total of 48 hours during the week. Her straight-time pay would be computed as follows:

An employee's *regular rate of pay* includes all the pay received for work performed during a seven-day period.

Category	Amount	Hours	Total
Hourly Rate	$10.00	48	$480.00
Shift Differential	$ 1.00	48	$ 48.00
Lead Worker	$ 1.25	48	$ 60.00
		Total	**$588.00**

Hue's regular rate of pay (overtime rate) is computed by dividing her total pay at straight time by the hours she worked as follows:

Hue's Total Pay	Divided by Hours Worked	Equals Regular Rate of Pay
$588.00	48	$12.25

Her regular rate of pay is $12.25. Her overtime rate is 1.5 times $12.25 or $18.38 per hour.

Hue's Regular Rate of Pay	Times 1.5	Equals Hue's Overtime Rate
$12.25	1.5	$18.38

Under the regular rate-of-pay formula, Hue is paid $12.25 per hour for the first 40 hours of work ($490). She is paid $18.38 for the eight hours of work over forty hours in the workweek ($147.04). Using the regular rate of pay, her total pay for the week is $637.04 as compared to the $588 we arrived at when we only used her hourly rate.

On-Call Time

A nonexempt employee is on call when you ask her to be available to work if she is needed. If you significantly limit the employee's freedom during this time, she is considered to be working.

Joan is an Emergency Technician at a local community hospital. The hospital tells Joan that they may need her over the weekend and that she needs to stay home so she can be called when she is needed.

Should the time Joan spends at home be considered work time?

For purposes of the FLSA, Joan is working because her freedom to move about is severely limited. If she is working, she must to be paid at least the minimum wage. However, if the hospital gives Joan a beeper and tells her that she must call in when the beeper sounds and then report to work within a reasonable time, she is not working and does not need to be paid for the time she is on call.

Training Time

Under the FLSA, a nonexempt employee must be paid for the time spent in training when the training is required by the employer. The training time is not considered work time and does not have to be paid time if the training is:

- Strictly voluntary.
- Occurs outside the employee's scheduled work hours.
- Results in no productive work.
- Is not directly related to the employee's job.

In other words, if you require a nonexempt employee to attend training, you must pay her for the time she is being trained. If the employee voluntarily attends training (e.g., night classes), she is not working, and you are not required to pay her. It is important for you to be clear on whether the employee is attending training on a voluntary or involuntary business. It is best to approve training in writing.

If you require a nonexempt employee to attend training, you must pay her for the time she is being trained.

Travel Time

If a nonexempt employee travels on public transportation during her normally scheduled work hours, the travel time is considered work time and must be paid. Even if the travel occurs on a day off, if it takes place during the employee's normally scheduled hours, it is considered work time. Travel time from home to the airport or other transportation terminal is not considered as work time. Once the employee arrives at her destination and is free to move about or is traveling after work hours (i.e., checked into the hotel), she is no longer working.

Driving from home to work and from work to home is not considered work time. However, traveling from one work site to another is considered work time and must be paid. If the employee drives on an out-of-town trip, the driving time (except meal periods) is considered working time, unless you have offered public transportation as an alternative.

Compensatory Time

If you offer a nonexempt employee time off rather than pay for overtime work, you are offering *compensatory time*. This type of arrangement is generally not permitted under the FLSA for nonexempt employees who work in the private sector. You should not allow nonexempt employees to accumulate comp time. You should pay them for all hours of work.

Comp time may be granted by public-sector employers only if it is given at the rate of time and one-half the number of hours worked (one and one-half hours for each hour of overtime worked). Public-sector employees may accrue up to 240 hours of comp time.

Penalties

An employer who fails to comply with the FLSA may be liable for penalties up to two times the back pay owed to the employee. The FLSA carries criminal penalties and requires an employer who loses a claim to pay the employee's attorney fees. In most instances, an FLSA investigation involves the employer's entire payroll, not just the moneys owed to an individual employee who files a complaint.

6

Steps for the Effective Supervisor

Here are some suggestions to help you implement the information in this chapter. If you use them, they will help you avoid legal problems. They will also help you manage people in a way that shows you respect them and appreciate their efforts and contributions.

Step 1— Follow the guidelines of your organization when making pay decisions. Hire new people in the lower end of established pay ranges. Unless an exception is carefully justified, assign only work that is described in the employee's job classification.

Step 2— Require nonexempt employees to record their work time. Pay nonexempt employees for all overtime hours worked. If appropriate, pay nonexempt employees for nonwork time such as on-call time, stand by time, and travel time.

Step 3—Set an example for nonexempt employees by arriving at work early, taking only the allotted time for lunch and breaks. Leave work at or after your scheduled time. In other words, don't take advantage of your exempt status to set yourself apart from hourly employees in a way that makes them feel like second-class members of the organization.

Chapter Six Review

Now that you have read Chapter Six, use this space to review what you have learned so far. If you are not sure of an answer, just refer to the text. **Answers appear on page 114.**

1. The Equal Pay Act of 1963 (choose one):
   a. Is an amendment to the Fair Labor Standards Act of 1938.
   b. Requires that men and women doing exactly the same job be paid exactly the same salary.
   c. Requires that men and women receive similar pay when they are performing work that is substantially similar or identical in skill, effort, and responsibility under similar working conditions.
   d. Answers a and b.
   e. Answers a and c.

2. The Fair Labor Standards Act of 1938 regulates overtime pay, the minimum wage, equal pay, and_____.

3. **True or False?**
   The *regular rate of pay* is the employee's hourly salary.

4. **True or False?**
   A nonexempt employee can give up her right to be paid overtime.

5. A nonexempt employee must be paid at least the minimum wage when she (choose one):

   a. Performs work that benefits the employer.
   b. Serves as a bona fide volunteer.
   c. Is on call and has limited freedom, such as having to wait by the phone.
   d. Voluntarily attends night classes on her own time.
   e. All of the above.
   f. Answers b and c.
   g. Answers a and c.

CHAPTER SEVEN

The Americans with Disabilities Act

Chapter Objectives

After reading this chapter and completing the exercises, you should be able to:

  Define disability.

  Understand and explain the concept of an essential function.

  Explain the role of reasonable accommodation in complying with the Americans with Disabilities Act.

José had a sinking feeling as he walked through the doorway. The receptionist stared at him as he walked toward her desk. He knew she was looking at his left leg. Even though his pants covered his brace, he was used to people looking at his leg rather than his face. He knew he was qualified for this job and he really wanted it. The look on the face of the receptionist, the stairway to the right of her desk, and the lack of an elevator told him he was going to have to overcome a lot of old stereotypes before he would have a fair shot at the job.

José walked up to the receptionist , put on his best smile, and said, "Hi, I'm José Gonzalez. I'm here for an interview with Honre Lefebre. How are you today?"

"I'm fine," she said. "I'll call Honre for you. I don't know where he's going to interview you, though. We don't have any interview rooms down here."

José smiled. "I'll be fine with the stairs," he said. He sat down hoping that Honre would be more open-minded than the receptionist.

An estimated 43 million Americans have some form of physical or mental disability. The Americans with Disabilities Act of 1990 (ADA) was adopted to promote and expand employment opportunities for this significant portion of the population.

ADA's Scope

The employment provisions of the ADA apply to employers with 15 or more employees. The ADA prohibits discrimination against individuals with physical or mental disabilities. It requires employers to reasonably accommodate disabilities for qualified applicants and employees. It applies to hiring, firing, benefits, and other terms and conditions of employment.

Defining a Disability

Under the ADA, a person is considered to have a disability if:

- He has a physical or mental disability that substantially limits one or more of the major life activities (a **current** disability).

- He has a record of an impairment that substantially limits one or more of the major life activities (a **previous** disability).

- He is regarded as having an impairment that substantially limits one or more of the major life activities (a **perceived** disability).

💡 **For Your Information**

Etiquette defines the proper way to interact with other people. We tend to define etiquette by our own experiences. If you grew up without a disability, you may not understand how a person with a disability wants you to interact with him or her. If you know someone who has a disability, ask that person if he or she would be willing to help you learn more about how people with a disability would like able-bodied people to interact with them. (If your friend would rather not share, don't press for information.)

Current Disabilities

Current, or known, disabilities include, but are not limited to, impairments caused by paralysis, blindness, deafness, and speech impediments. They include cerebral palsy, epilepsy, muscular dystrophy, multiple sclerosis, cancer, heart disease, diabetes, mental retardation, emotional illness, HIV, tuberculosis, and other illnesses. They can include both contagious and noncontagious diseases.

Previous Disabilities

The second disability category includes impairments that may or may not be currently active but, if taken into consideration, may have a negative impact on employment decisions. Consider the following example:

An employee was treated for cancer several years ago. The cancer is in remission. The employee applies for promotion to a position that involves travel, extended work hours, and supervision of ten employees. The supervisor decides not to promote the employee out of concern that the additional stress of the higher-level position would cause the cancer to return.

Has the supervisor discriminated?

The supervisor has discriminated against the employee on the basis of a past disability. The employee's previous medical condition should not be a factor in making such an employment decision. The supervisor is not qualified to evaluate the employee's medical condition. If the employee is otherwise qualified for the job and the cancer becomes a factor, the ADA requires the employer to reasonably accommodate the condition.

Perceived Disabilities

Perceived disabilities include conditions that are not necessarily a medical disability but cause the applicant or employee to be treated in a discriminatory manner. An example might be disfigurement from burns or cosmetic appearance, such as a birthmark. A decision to pass over an otherwise qualified applicant or employee for a job assignment because the employer thinks that person is disabled, even if he or she is not, is discriminatory under the ADA.

A Qualified Individual

Like the other equal employment laws that came before it, the ADA does not require an employer to hire or promote a person who is not qualified to do the job. Under the ADA, however, a person is qualified if he can perform the **essential functions** of the job with or without a **reasonable accommodation.**

Essential Job Functions

The first step in complying with the ADA is to carefully define the job to be performed. The ADA introduced a new concept in job descriptions called *essential functions*. An essential function is a job duty that must be performed. In most cases, it is the main reason the position was created. It might also be a job duty that is not performed frequently, but is critical to the position.

A police officer's use of a gun is an example of an essential job function. Although the officer might not use the gun for weeks, months, or even years, the ability to use the gun on a moment's notice is an essential job function for the officer.

An essential job function might also be one that must be performed due to the limited size of an employer's staff.

Within a small mail-order firm, all employees might need to be able to process customer orders, no matter what their other specific job duties might be.

An *essential function* is a job duty that must be performed.

7

93

Nonessential functions, on the other hand, are those that make up only a small portion of the job. Under the ADA, you may not give significant weight to nonessential functions.

How would you weigh the following duties for an Administrative Assistant position?

40%	Research information for reports
30%	Schedule and coordinate meetings
25%	Key customer contacts
5%	Typing reports

Because of the amount of time spent and the importance of the first three duties, they would be considered essential functions. Typing reports, however, appears to be a minor part of the job. Typing is not an essential function. The ability to type cannot be a consideration in selecting a candidate under the ADA.

✔ Self-Check

List the essential functions of your job. How much time do you spend on each group of job duties? Which duties do you consider to be essential?

Job Duties	% of Time
_____	_____
_____	_____
_____	_____

With or Without a Reasonable Accommodation

The ADA requires that employees make reasonable accommodation for qualified job candidates. In other words, if an applicant is qualified to do the work, he or she should be a viable candidate for the job. If a reasonable accommodation is necessary to help the candidate perform the duties, it should not prevent the candidate from getting the job. A reasonable accommodation could be as simple as raising a desk to allow a wheelchair to fit underneath it, or as complex as installing an elevator to allow access to upper floors. It could involve changing work hours to allow the use of public transportation, or it might require a second employee to assist a sight-impaired employee in some aspect of the job.

An accommodation is required under the ADA only if it is a reasonable accommodation. The magnitude and cost of the accommodation along with the size and resources of the employer must be taken into consideration to decide whether an accommodation is reasonable. For example, buying a $15,000 computer to accommodate a sight-impaired person might be reasonable for a large electronics manufacturer but unreasonable for a small photography studio.

For Your Information

The ADA's requirements extend to job applicants. Look around your Human Resources office and the areas you use for interviewing and testing. Would an applicant with a physical or mental disability have access to your facilities without an unreasonable restriction? What steps could be taken to ensure that access for those with disabilities is equal to those without disabilities?

7

Steps for the Effective Supervisor

Here are some suggestions to help you implement the information in this chapter. If you use them, they will help you avoid legal problems. They will also help you manage people in a way that shows you respect them and appreciate their efforts and contributions.

Step 1— Call your local chapter of the Easter Seal Society or another group that represents people with disabilities to learn more about helping people with disabilities to be productive members of your workforce. Ask one of their representatives to make a presentation to your department.

Step 2— Review job descriptions in your department to be sure they are job-related from the perspective of the Americans with Disabilities Act. Remove language that requires employees to be totally free of a disability when a reasonable accommodation could be made.

Step 3— Ask Human Resources to explain the policy for helping or working with employees who become disabled. For example, what is your leave policy? Do you have a "light duty" program? How can you restructure jobs to reasonably accommodate disabled employees?

Chapter Seven Review

Now that you have read Chapter Seven, use this space to review what you have learned so far. **Answers appear on page 115.**

1. A disability can be (choose one):

   a. Physical

   b. Mental

   c. Both

2. **True or False?**
   Under the ADA, a disability can be a current disability, a previous disability, or a perceived disability.

3. What does the term essential functions mean?

   _____

   _____

   _____

4. When you hire a disabled person, you must (choose one):

   a. Do whatever it takes to change the job, the facility, or the working conditions to allow the employee to work for you.

   b. Make reasonable accommodations so that the qualified candidate can perform the essential functions of the position.

   c. Tell everyone to pretend that the person does not have a disability.

CHAPTER EIGHT

Other Employment Laws

Chapter Objectives

After reading this chapter and completing the exercises, you should be able to:

 Discuss the general concepts of several federal employment laws.

 Review a personnel file to identify information that should be kept in the file.

 Ask questions to learn more about employment laws in your state.

Ralph couldn't believe what he'd just heard. In order to qualify for large government contracts, his company was going to become an affirmative action employer. "I'd hate to see us do that," Ralph said. "Wouldn't that mean we'd have to hire whoever the government told us to instead of the most qualified person for the job?"

The list of laws and legal principles that affect employment can seem never-ending. So far, we have discussed some of the more frequently referenced federal laws. In this chapter we will briefly review a variety of other federal and state employment laws and regulations.

Affirmative Action

Affirmative action in employment was created on September 24, 1965, when President Lyndon Johnson signed Executive Order 11246. (An executive order is a policy statement signed by the president.) Executive Order 11246 requires government contractors and subcontractors with 50 or more employees and more than $50,000 in federal government business to be affirmative-action employers. (Some state and local governments have a similar requirement.)

An employer who has fewer than 50 employees or contracts or subcontracts for less than $50,000 in federal government-related business is not required to be an affirmative-action employer. In other words, an employer has a choice about whether it wants to be an affirmative-action employer. If the employer does not want to be an affirmative-action employer, it does not have to contract or subcontract federal government-related business. It must, however, comply with other equal-employment laws such as the Civil Rights Act of 1964.

What Is Affirmative Action?

The word *affirmative* means to state agreement. The word *action* means to consciously do something. An affirmative-action employer agrees to take positive steps to invite minorities and women to participate as full members of the workplace. These steps involve:

- Studying the *availability* of minorities and women in the community.
- Comparing the workforce at all levels of the organization to the availability of qualified minorities and women in the community.
- Working to balance the makeup of the workforce with the availability of qualified minorities and women in the community.
- Ensuring that employment openings are well-publicized in the community in a way that makes them available to potential minority and female candidates.
- Ensuring that employment policies and practices do not create discriminatory practices.

8

The basic premise of affirmative action is that women and minorities do not have the same access to employment as other members of the community. The goal of affirmative action is to have employers reach out to the community to seek and include women and minorities in the workplace.

💡 For Your Information

The Office of Federal Contract Compliance Programs (OFCCP) periodically audits affirmative-action employers. The audit can be a result of a random process the OFCCP uses to select employers for an audit, or it may result from an employee complaint. It can also be part of an OFCCP program to audit contractors or subcontractors in an industry or area.

Executive order 11246 is enforced by the United States Department of Labor, Office of Federal Contract Compliance Programs (OFCCP). Affirmative action does not require employers to hire unqualified workers. It does require employers to seek out and consider qualified female and minority candidates. By seeking out qualified candidates, the employer increases the diversity of the applicant pool. The larger the number of qualified minorities and women represented in the applicant pool, the more they are likely to be selected.

If the OFCCP finds that an employer is not meeting its affirmative action commitments, it first works to reach an agreement with the employer to correct the situation. If an agreement cannot be reached, or if the employer does not meet its obligations under an agreement, the OFCCP can stop payment on the contract. It can also pull the contract from the employer. The OFCCP can also place the employer on a "no bid" list to prohibit it from receiving other work from the federal government. Finally, the OFCCP can refer the matter to the Justice Department to file a federal lawsuit against the employer.

✔ Self-Check

If your company is an affirmative-action employer, ask to see the affirmative-action plan. After reading it, work with Human Resources to answer the following questions:

- ■ Does your department's workforce reflect the nature of your community?

- ■ If it does not, what recruitment methods will allow you to attract and retain qualified women and minorities?

The Family and Medical Leave Act of 1993

Employers with 50 or more employees within a 75-mile radius of each other are covered by the federal Family and Medical Leave Act (FMLA). Under the FMLA, an employee may request time off for:

■ The birth, adoption, or foster care placement of a child.

■ The employee's own serious illness.

■ The serious illness of a parent, child, or spouse.

An employee is eligible for FMLA leave if he or she has worked for the employer for at least 12 months and has worked at least 1,250 hours in the 12 months before the leave starts. An employer is not required to provide an FMLA leave to certain key employees. A key employee is a salaried employee who is among the top ten percent of the highest-paid employees within a 75-mile radius.

An FMLA leave can be for up to 12 weeks in a 12-month period. The 12 weeks do not have to be consecutive. For example, if an employee requires periodic treatment or examinations, the time required for those visits may be counted toward an FMLA leave.

Employer's Responsibilities

It is the employer's responsibility to notify the employee of his or her right to take an FMLA leave. The employer may ask the employee to provide enough information, including confirmation from a physician, to verify that the leave request qualifies under the FMLA. Keep in mind, however, that information about an individual's medical condition is considered confidential. As a result, you do not normally need to know the specific medical condition that is involved. In addition, you must not share any medical information you obtain with other people unless they have a legitimate business need to know the information.

An employee is eligible for FMLA leave if he or she has worked for the employer for at least 12 months and has worked at least 1,250 hours in the 12 months before the leave starts.

8

Generally, an FMLA leave is without pay. However, an employee may use sick leave or accrued vacation time, with approval, during an FMLA leave. The employer is required to continue paying its share of health insurance premiums during an FMLA leave and to keep the employee's group health insurance in force even if it requires advancing money for coverage.

When an employee returns from an FMLA leave, he or she is entitled to return to the same position, or a substantially similar position. In effect, the employee cannot lose any status (including pay, benefits, seniority, and other employment rights) as a result of taking an FMLA leave. If the employee returns from the FMLA leave with a condition that is a recognized disability, you may need to consider making a reasonable accommodation as required by the Americans with Disabilities Act.

If an employee in your department needs to take an FMLA leave, you should be sure that she or he is referred to Human Resources. Human Resources should inform the employee of his or her rights and require the employee to fill out a leave request form. If the employee is not able to report to Human Resources, arrangements should be made to take or mail the information to the employee.

COBRA

The Consolidated Omnibus Budget Reconciliation Act of 1985 (COBRA) requires employers with 20 or more employees to allow eligible employees to continue their group health insurance coverage after their employment ends, or if their work hours are reduced to a point that they lose coverage, at their own expense. COBRA also allows qualified beneficiaries (e.g., spouse and dependent children) to continue their coverage after it is discontinued by the policy provisions (e.g., death of a parent, parent becoming eligible for Medicare, divorce, dependent losing dependent status under the plan rules, or termination of the employee's employment).

COBRA requires employers with 20 or more employees to allow eligible employees to continue their group health insurance coverage after their employment ends, or if their work hours are reduced to a point that they lose coverage, at their own expense.

Length of Coverage

An eligible employee or dependent may continue coverage for up to 18 months if she or he becomes eligible for COBRA coverage due to termination of the employee's employment or a reduction in hours. If a beneficiary becomes eligible, he or she may be eligible to continue coverage for up to 36 months. The covered individual must elect to be covered by COBRA within 60 days after the insurance coverage ends following a qualifying event or within 60 days after the date a beneficiary is sent a notice to select coverage. The covered individual must pay the premium costs for the insurance. The employer may add an administrative charge of up to 2 percent to the premium.

If an employee in your department leaves the company, be sure that Human Resources is notified. Human Resources should notify the employee of his or her rights under COBRA. Likewise, if the status of an employee's spouse or dependent changes in a way that might make that person eligible for COBRA, Human Resources should be notified.

The Drug-Free Workplace Act of 1988

If an employer contracts with the federal government for the procurement of property or services valued at more than $25,000, the employer must certify that it will provide a drug-free workplace. The certification must include a plan for ensuring a drug-free workplace. The plan must include certain elements, such as employee education, establishing compliance with the program as a condition of employment, and taking appropriate disciplinary action against employees who violate the policy.

In addition to the Drug-Free Workplace Act of 1988, the Department of Transportation and the Department of Defense have issued regulations that require covered employers to conduct random drug tests and maintain certain records. You should check with Human Resources to see if your company is covered by these regulations and take steps to be sure that you comply with them.

In most states, pre-employment drug testing is acceptable because an applicant has a choice of whether or not to seek employment from a specific employer.

8

Drug Testing

Drug testing is a complex employment issue. Employers have an interest in keeping illegal drugs out of the workplace. On the other hand, employees are protected from an unnecessary invasion of their privacy.

Drug testing is generally controlled by state laws. In most states, pre-employment drug testing is acceptable because an applicant has a choice of whether or not to seek employment from a specific employer.

States vary in their approach to postemployment drug testing. In some states, random drug testing of employees is permissible. In others, it is not. In many states, reasonable suspicion drug testing is permitted. Reasonable suspicion exists when an employer has reached an independent conclusion that an employee's ability to function in the workplace is impaired. This is usually done by having more than one supervisor observe an employee for objective signs of an impairment.

You should always check with Human Resources and your labor attorney before requiring a drug test. Like other tests, a drug test is more legally defensible when it is based on an objective job-related reason.

The Immigration Reform and Control Act of 1986

The Immigration Reform and Control Act (IRCA) requires all employers to verify that employees hired after November 6, 1986, are eligible to work in the United States. The law carries serious penalties for employers who knowingly hire, refer, recruit, or retain employees who are not authorized to work in the United States.

Under the IRCA, an employee must complete an I-9 form within the first three days of employment. The I-9 form allows employees to present various documents (such as a Social Security card or birth certificate) to prove that they are legally qualified to work within the United States. The employer is required to inspect the documents presented by the employee and certify that they appear to be legitimate documents.

The Immigration Reform and Control Act (IRCA) requires all employers to verify that employees hired after November 6, 1986, are eligible to work in the United States

An employer may not discriminate against a job candidate on the basis of citizenship or national origin. Therefore, all employees must complete an I-9 form. If an employee is not able to provide proper documentation within three days of employment, he or she may not continue working. In some cases, proper documentation may include a receipt showing that the employee has applied for documents.

The National Labor Relations Act

The National Labor Relations Act (NLRA) of 1935 guarantees employees the right to organize, join, and participate in labor unions. The NLRA is administered by the National Labor Relations Board. The NLRA also gives employees the right to not participate in labor union activities. You may not discriminate against an employee because he or she is involved in union activities.

Employees often decide to form or join a union because they believe management has been unfair. Their belief may result from the treatment of one supervisor. It may stem from a perception that working conditions or salaries are unfair. It may be over a concern for job security.

A rumor is often the first sign of a union-organizing campaign. If you hear employees talking about a union, you should notify Human Resources. You should not try to talk employees out of joining a union or hold their interest in a union against them in any way. Human Resources will work with the company's legal staff to plan a response to the union's efforts to organize employees.

For Your Information

During a union-organizing campaign, the union asks employees to sign an "authorization card." Signing the card is like signing a power of attorney. It gives the union the right to represent the employee in matters related to wages, hours, and working conditions.

If the union collects cards from 30 percent of the employees in a potential bargaining unit, they can ask for an election. If the union collects cards from 50 percent + 1 employee in the bargaining unit, they may ask the NLRB to certify the union as the bargaining agent for the employees without an election.

If an employee signs a card and then decides she or he does not want to be represented by the union, she or he must write to the union to rescind the card. As a supervisor, you should never handle or inquire about union cards.

8

During a union-organizing campaign, you may express your opinions about unions. You may talk about your experiences with unions and discuss facts related to unions. You may not threaten or intimidate employees, make promises to employees, or spy on employees with respect to union-organizing activities. If you violate employee rights during an organizing campaign, the union may file an unfair labor practice charge that can result in the union being recognized without an election. If an election is held and a union is recognized, the union gains the right to represent employees and the right to bargain with management.

Personnel Records

Most of the laws we have discussed in this book include requirements for maintaining files and information. Each law includes specific provisions. The law often varies as to the length of time records must be kept. You should always check with your Human Resources or employment law advisor before discarding recruitment, performance evaluation, progressive discipline, personnel, payroll, safety, or other employment records.

In addition to maintaining accurate records, you must also control access to personnel files. Most states have a law that allows an employee to inspect his or her personnel file upon reasonable notice during normal business hours. There should not be any surprises in an employee's personnel file. When employees ask to see their personnel files, they should only find information that they already know.

A personnel file should not contain information that can be used to discriminate against an employee. For example, an employee's picture can show age, gender, race, color, physical condition, and other information that could influence a personnel decision. If an employer decides to keep a picture of an employee, it should be kept in a security file separate from the personnel file. Health insurance information, worker's compensation information, marital status, age, information about dependents, and other such information should be kept separate from the personnel file.

Workplace Violence

A new and expanding area in employment law is workplace violence. Recent studies indicate that homicide is the number two cause of death in the workplace. For women, homicide is the number one cause of death in the workplace.

✔ Self-Check

Does your organization have a plan for dealing with workplace violence? If it does, be sure that you know what should be done in the event of a threat or actual violence. If it doesn't have a plan, consider forming a committee to develop one.

The Occupational Health and Safety Act (OSHA) includes a General Duty Clause that holds employers responsible for providing a safe workplace even when there are no regulations for employers to follow. Workplace violence falls into this category. Employers should take special care to survey the workplace to ensure that reasonable efforts have been taken to minimize the risk of violence. Doors and entrances should be properly secured. Name tags, visitor logs and, other access-control steps should be implemented. Reference checks and background checks should be completed on new employees to be sure they are who they say they are and that they have the experience and education they claim to have.

Supervisors and employees should be trained to recognize employee, customer, and visitor behaviors that may signal potential violence. If possible, an employee assistance program should be in place to allow supervisors to refer troubled employees for professional assistance. Most important, employees at all levels must understand that threats and intimidation will be viewed as a serious matter and meet with serious disciplinary action up to and including termination.

California has recently enacted regulations requiring employers to adopt a written workplace-violence plan. The state has also published a model plan for California employers.

8

The Polygraph Protection Act of 1988

The Polygraph Protection Act of 1988 severely restricts the use of lie-detector tests for employment-related purposes. Because of the very limited circumstances under which such tests may be used, you should consult with legal counsel before considering their use. In addition, you may not discipline, discharge, or discriminate against an employee or job applicant who refuses to take a lie-detector test.

State and Local Laws

Throughout this book, we have focused on federal employment laws. You should also research local and state employment laws that affect your workplace. For example:

- In Michigan, employers may not discriminate on the basis of height and weight.

- In Washington, D.C., employers may not discriminate on the basis of matriculation.

- In California, employers may not discriminate on the basis of sexual orientation, HIV, AIDS, ancestry, marital status, or cancer.

- In addition, many local governments have adopted laws regulating smoking, gambling, soliciting, and other activities in the workplace.

Posting and Notice Requirements

Many of the federal laws we have discussed require employers to post notices explaining that the employer is covered by the law. These notices must be visible (i.e., not covered by other documents) and up-to-date. In some cases, failure to post these notices can result in criminal penalties for the employer. At the very least, failing to post the notices sends a message that the employer does not take its obligations under the law seriously. You should check to be sure that these posters are visible and up-to-date in each of your work locations.

Conclusion

This book has given you an overview of some of the more frequently referenced laws and legal principles that affect your relationship with employees. It is intended as a starting point in your effort to learn more about your responsibilities as a supervisor. You should take time to learn more by attending classes, seminars, and workshops. We encourage you to continue to read articles and other books to expand your knowledge base. You should talk with your company's human resources and labor law experts to learn as much as you can about your responsibilities and obligations as a supervisor.

Steps for the Effective Supervisor

Here are some suggestions to help you implement the information in this chapter. If you use them, they will help you avoid legal problems. They will also help you manage people in a way that shows you respect them and appreciate their efforts and contributions.

Step 1— Ask Human Resources if your organization is an affirmative-action employer. If it is, read the plan and ask questions to help you understand it.

Step 2— Become familiar with company policies for various types of medical, maternity, and personal leaves. When you talk to an employee about a leave, be sure your answers reflect the requirements of the policy. Treat a leave-of-absence request as a business issue. Deal with it objectively and fairly. Avoid derogatory, demeaning, or negative comments about an employee's request.

Step 3— When an employee leaves the organization, notify your benefits representative to be sure the employee is notified of his or her COBRA rights.

Step 4— Communicate to employees that drugs and alcohol do not belong in the workplace. Enforce polices that prohibit drugs and alcohol. Set a personal example by drinking nonalcoholic beverages at parties and celebrations.

Step 5— Avoid disparaging comments about the national origin or citizenship of others.

Step 6— If you learn of union-organizing activity in your department or organization, notify Human Resources immediately.

Step 7— Give an employee a copy of anything you put in her or his personnel file.

Step 8— Express a zero-tolerance policy for threats in the workplace. Seek help from Human Resources and/or the Employee Assistance Program to address stress problems, threats, or other potentially dangerous acts in the workplace.

Chapter Eight Review

Now that you have read Chapter Eight, use this space to review what you have learned so far. If you are not sure of an answer, just refer to the text. **Answers appear on page 115.**

1. **True or False?**
   Every employee in every company is eligible for family and medical leave.

2. IRCA requires (choose one):

   a. Employers to verify that a new employee is eligible to work in the United States.

   b. Employers to verify that the employee has documentation to satisfy the requirements explained on the I-9 form.

   c. Employers to verify that a new employee is a United States citizen.

3. **True or False?**
   The number one cause of death in the workplace is homicide.

4. **True or False?**
   You should take out any embarrassing or sensitive information before you show an employee her or his personnel file.

Suggested Answers to Exercises

Chapter One

(from page 17)

1. a. Fair and consistent supervisors are less likely to be sued.

2. Everything the supervisor says and does represents the company.

3. Establishing a grievance procedure.
   Establishing a complaint procedure.

4. b. HR can advise you on how to handle a variety of situations.

5. Speak confidentially to your attorney.

Chapter Two

(from page 27)

1. Race, sex, religion, national origin, color

2. A category defined in a federal or state law that may not be used to make an employment decision unless a bona fide occupational qualification exists.

3. **1972** Added coverage for state and local government agencies.
   1978 Added the Pregnancy Discrimination Act.
   1991 Allowed plaintiffs to obtain jury trials and punitive damages in federal court.

4. Intentional

5. Unintentional

6. Holding against a person her or his exercise of a right to file a discrimination harassment, or sexual harassment claim.

7. A decision that is based on objective information that is reasonably related to the work assignments of a position.

Chapter Three

(from page 43)

1. False

2. Verbal, physical, visual

3. Situations where a supervisor uses his or her power to gain sexual favors from an employee.

4. Situations and behaviors that affect the workplace in a manner that creates an intimidating, hostile, or offensive environment.

5. In a negative way to gain sexual favors and create a hostile work environment.
   In a positive way to create a productive workplace environment.

Chapter Four

(from page 63)

1. True

2. Job-related

3. b. Asking job-related questions that encourage the employee to talk about specific past experiences to help you predict his or her future performance.

4. 40

5. f. Answers c and d.

Chapter Five

(from page 77)

1. At any time with or without notice for any reason, or for any reason, so long as it is not an unlawful reason.

2. Reduction in force or lay off
   Violation of a rule
   Inability or failure to perform

3. False

4. c. It creates an opportunity for the employee to be successful.

Chapter Six

(from page 89)

1. e. Answers a and c.

2. Child labor

3. False

4. False

5. g. Answers a and c.

Chapter Seven

(from page 97)

1. c. Both

2. True

3. An essential function is a job duty that must be performed by the position. It might also be a job duty that is not performed frequently, but is critical to the position. An essential function might also be one that must be performed by the employee due to the limited size of an employer's staff.

4. b. Make reasonable accommodations so that the qualified candidate can perform the essential functions of the position.

Chapter Eight

(from page 111)

1. False

2. b. Employers to verify that the employee has documentation to satisfy the requirements explained on the I-9 form.

3. False

4. False

Glossary

Affirmative Action—a proactive program by an employer to analyze the community and the workforce to identify underutilization and take steps to increase the representation of women and minorities in the workforce; required of government contractors and subcontractors who have 50 or more employees and do $50,000 annual business with the federal government.

Applicant Pool—the group of people who apply or could apply for an employment opening.

Attorney-Client Privilege—the right of an attorney and a client to discuss issues without having to reveal their discussion to other people.

At-Will Employment—the basic employment right of an employer to hire and terminate employees and the right of an employee to enter into or end an employment relationship.

Availability—an affirmative-action term to describe the number or percentage of qualified women and minorities in the community as defined by the eight-factor analysis.

Behavioral Interviewing—a concept pioneered by Dr. Paul Green that focuses the interview on specific past behavior to obtain information that reasonably predicts future behavior.

Compensatory Time—allowing a nonexempt employee to accumulate time off for future personal use instead of being paid for overtime worked; prohibited by the Fair Labor Standards Act, except in the public sector.

Complaint Procedure—a formal method for employees to use to bring problems, such as sexual harassment, to the attention of management. (A complaint procedure differs from a grievance in that it does not have steps for appealing a decision.)

Discrimination—negative treatment, or a negative result, that is based on membership in a protected group.

Disparate Treatment—treating employees in a protected class differently from other employees.

Disparate Impact—actions based on a neutral policy that results in an adverse impact on a protected group or individual.

EEO-1 Categories—Officials and Managers, Professionals, Technicians, Sales Workers, Office and Clerical, Craft Workers (skilled), Operatives (semiskilled), Laborers (unskilled), Formal On-the-Job Trainees as defined by the EEOC.

Eight-Factor Analysis—a statistical analysis of the community to determine the availability of qualified women and minorities.

Employment Decisions—hire and promote, discipline and terminate, assign work and responsibilities, train, coach and counsel, establish terms (length) of employment, establish conditions (circumstances) of employment, or establish privileges (benefits) of employment.

Environmental Sexual Harassment—conduct based on gender or sex that unreasonably interferes with an individual's work performance or has the purpose or effect of creating an intimidating, hostile, or offensive work environment.

Epithet—a word, phrase, or statement that labels or stereotypes a person based on her or his membership in a protected group.

Essential Functions—an ADA term to describe a job duty that must be performed by the position, or a job duty that is not performed frequently but is critical to the position, or a job duty that must be performed by the position due to the limited size of an employer's staff.

Exempt Employee—a salaried employee who is not eligible for overtime because his or her position is classified as executive, administrative, professional, etc., as defined by the Fair Labor Standards Act.

General Duty Clause—a provision in the Occupational Safety and Health Act that holds employers liable for unsafe workplace conditions even if a regulation is not in place to control the employer's actions.

Implied Contract—actions or statements that lead one of the parties to an employment contract to believe that unstated promises exist.

Implied Covenant of Good Faith and Fair Dealing—a promise implied by law that neither party to a contract will interfere with the other party's ability to perform the contract. With regard to employment contracts, long-term employment, good performance evaluations, pay raises, and other positive job factors, it is implied that termination will only be for good cause.

Introductory Period or **Training Period**—the initial period of employment as defined by the employer.

Job-Related—information that reasonably predicts the success on the job; information that is reasonably related to the job and allows the employer to make a reasonable, objective employment decision.

Knew or Should Have Known—a phrase that is often used to describe a company's liability for environmental sexual harassment; it means that the company will be held responsible if it ignores a known situation or if it does not pay attention and take action with regard to a behavior that was inappropriate in the workplace.

Negligent Hiring—employment of a person who is not qualified or who possesses characteristics that are considered dangerous and results in harm or injury to another party.

Nonexempt Employee—an employee who is eligible for overtime under the provisions of the Fair Labor Standards Act.

Personnel File—a confidential file that contains information used to make employment decisions about an employee.

Probation Period—a set period of time during which the employer clearly retains its at-will employment rights; frequently, the initial employment period defined in a union contract.

Progressive Discipline—a defined set of steps that normally includes training, counseling, oral warning, verbal warning, last-step option, and termination; the steps may be bypassed in the event of a serious violation of company rules or failure to perform a critical job duty.

Protected Groups—categories identified by state or federal law that may not be used to make employment decisions unless a bona fide occupational qualification exists.

Quid Pro Quo Sexual Harassment—this for that; something for something; sexual harassment that involves one party using power over another to gain some sort of sexual advantage.

Reasonable Accommodation—an ADA term to explain that an employer must first decide whether an employee is qualified to do the work and then make cost-effective changes to the workplace to accommodate a disabled individual.

Reclassify—reassigning an employee's position from one job title or classification to another because the employee's job duties have changed; a reclassification may move the employee to a job title that pays a higher, a lower, or the same salary as the employee is currently making.

Reduction in Force—an objective decision to lay off employees due to a change in technology that eliminates the need for the employee's position, or requires a new set of skills that the employee does not possess and cannot obtain in a reasonable period of time; or the elimination of a position for organizational, financial or other legitimate business reasons; or a decision to combine the duties of one or more positions to reduce overhead or eliminate duplication of effort.

Regular Rate of Pay—the employee's total productivity-related pay divided by the total number of hours worked in a seven-day period; used to compute overtime pay under the FLSA.

Retaliation—holding against a person, directly or indirectly, her or his right to complain about violations of federal or state law or public policy.

Sexual Harassment—unlawful use of sexual behavior in the workplace (see quid pro quo and environmental).

Strictly Liable—a concept often applied in quid pro quo sexual harassment cases that means because there is no excuse for the behavior, the company and/or the supervisor will be held responsible for their action or inaction.

Subterfuge Termination—telling a person he or she is being released from employment for one reason when actually another reason is being used.

Term, Condition or Privilege of Employment—the circumstances under which an employment relationship is established and carried out.

Underrepresentation—an affirmative-action term to explain that the percentage of women or minorities in the workforce of an employer does not balance with the available population of qualified women or minorities in the community.

Violation of Public Policy—a concept that places the safety and interests of the general public ahead of the rights of employers to hire and terminate employees.

Walk the Talk—a phrase employees use to explain their belief that supervisors should do what they say they are going to do.

With or Without a Reasonable Accommodation—an ADA term to explain that an employment decision should be made on the basis of a person's qualifications; if the person is qualified and disabled, the employer must make cost-effective changes to the workplace to accommodate the disability.

Workplace Violence—any act, statement, or condition that places employees, visitors, and facilities in the workplace in a situation that may result in emotional or physical danger, harm, or death.

Wrongful Termination—voluntary or involuntary separation from employment that violates a statute, a public policy, or an express or implied employment contract.